WHEN YOU HEAR ME

(YOU HEAR US)

Voices on Youth Incarceration

Free Minds Book Club & Writing Workshop

Foreword by Shaka Senghor

ISBN: 9781950807345 (paperback) / 9781950807369 (hardcover)

Cover Art by Ricardo Levins Morales
Photography by KK Ottesen
Design by Gigi Mascarenas

Free Minds Editorial Team
Tara Libert, Executive Director
Julia Mascioli, Managing Editor
Kelli Taylor, Interviewer and Editor
KK Ottesen, Interviewer and Editor

Free Minds Book Club & Writing Workshop is a DC-based nonprofit organization that works with incarcerated and formerly incarcerated youths and adults, using the literary arts, workforce development, trauma healing, and advocacy to create personal and societal change.

Shout Mouse Press is a nonprofit writing and publishing program dedicated to amplifying underheard voices. Learn more and see our full catalog at www.shoutmousepress.org

Shout Mouse Press, 1638 R Street NW, Suite 218, Washington, DC 20009
Trade distribution: Ingram Publisher Services International

For information about special discounts and bulk purchases, please contact Shout Mouse Press sales at 240-772-1545 or orders@shoutmousepress.org.

The poem "Mother" was first published in the book *Poetry and Art: Visions from Inside* (Keven McIntyre, Cadmus Publishing).

The poem "Dear America" was previously published in *Iron City Magazine* (2018).

The poem "I Will Cry for the Little Boy" was previously published in *Tacenda Literary Magazine* (2017).

The poem "A Cell" was previously published by the Academy of American Poets as part of the Poem-A-Day series on Poets.Org.

The poem "Staring at the Wall" was previously published in *Tacenda Literary Magazine* (2016).

The poem "I Know Pain" was previously published in *Tacenda Literary Magazine* (2015).

The poem "Sometimes I Cry" was previously published by the Academy of American Poets as part of the Poem-A-Day series on Poets.Org.

The poem "A poem from a father to his youngest son" was previously published by the Academy of American Poets as part of the Poem-A-Day series on Poets.Org.

Dedicated to the legacy of Free Minds members we have lost:

James, Cortez, Derrick, Christian, JohnQuan, Nadar, Andre, Darond, Dontel, Tyree, Antwone, Amari, Kuron, Dwayne, Darnell, Marcus, Wayne, Eric, Sharod, Arthur, Isaiah H., DeMario, Mshairi, Tahlil, Donta, Joshua, John, Delonte, Eddie, Gary, Benny, Michael, David, Navaras, Dewayne, Tyrone, Darius, Aaron, Harold, Isaiah A.

And to all who are committed to using the literary arts to heal and transform the lives and communities of those most impacted by the traumas of violence and incarceration. May this book be a tool to guide us to a reimagined future with true accountability and transformative justice.

And to the original Free Mind:

Glen

Table of Contents

THE WAR THAT REPLAYS IN MY MIND
(GROWING UP)

TRAPPED
(IMPRISONMENT)

THE LAND OF BROKEN SOULS
(SOLITARY CONFINEMENT)

WHEN THE SKY BLINKS
(LOVE)

I KNOW PAIN
(EMOTIONS)

TAKIN' LOSSES
(GRIEF)

I FORGIVE ME
(TRANSFORMATION)

FOR THE TIME LOST
(FAMILY)

LIFE AFTER INCARCERATION
(REENTRY)

WRITING MY WAY OUT
(RESISTANCE)

Foreword

My first true love affair started when I was 19 years old. I will never forget that day or that moment. I was at Carson City Correctional Facility in Michigan. It was a frostbit January afternoon when I walked into the library. It was there that I met my love.

Her pages were dog-eared and her opening paragraphs enigmatic. But her soul beckoned, so I heeded her call. I was a young kid, fresh on the set, forgotten by the world and mentally stressed. She wasn't having it. She first snatched my eyes wide open with tales by Donald Goines, who wrote bold depictions of life on the streets. I was falling madly in love and was blindsided by what happened next. Before you knew it I was reading powerful jewels about Garvey, Nat Turner, and Malcolm X. I thought to myself, *Damn in the middle of a torturous environment, I found a true blessing.*

The things that I didn't think really mattered, now mattered, in ways I couldn't have imagined. Instead of hustling to fill my pockets, and stepping through streets full of empty shells and blood splatter, I was focused on elevated conversations, and ducking idle chatter. It wasn't long before I realized that with her, there was nothing that could stop me.

My love took me on trips from the Antarctic to the banks of the Nile. She hugged me with Zora Neale Hurston, had me wishing I would have met her in person. Her imagery had me thirsting for more words of power, topics I could devour, blazing through pages, hour after hour, day after day, night after night, teaching myself so I could see right. Before her I had seen way too much wrong—I mean Toni Morrison wrote about it in Solomon's song.

She had me open, no longer feeling hopeless. She got me focused on the bigger picture, Harlem Renaissance literature. No longer a minor leaguer, I found out—in the grand scheme of life—we were *major* figures. I became visible reading Ralph Ellison, Claude Brown, Countee Cullen, James Baldwin. This love of mine, she introduced me to them, and they decided to welcome me in.

Her friends carved legacies: Langston Hughes, Gloria Naylor, Jean Toomer. All of their styles were wild, like grass or blues or jazz, tempo just right, not too slow or too fast. I connected with her people and kept on going, word after word, scribe after scribe, book after book—she truly had me hooked.

So yes, to escape the hellish existence of 19 years in prison, I fell in love with books. Books that challenged me, evolved me, and deepened my sense of purpose. Most importantly books that led me to become a lover of words and their power to shift us, transport us, and create a portal into a world of freedom.

This is why the poems and stories in this book are so important: these authors, scribes, poets, and architects of wordplay give up their souls to inspire our hearts. They don't write to make you feel happy, safe, or hopeful; they write, because if they don't, they will die from suffocating, from the feeling of being trampled. They write to mirror back to us the bullsh*t we say to make people feel good about the scraps of time we loan to these experiences. They write because it affirms their greatness and creativity—not for us but for them. We are just lucky to be counted amongst those who get a chance to witness, to receive these offerings.

As you read this beautiful collection, I hope you find yourself falling in love with the power of the page, the way I did many, many years ago.

— Shaka Senghor

Author of *Writing My Wrongs: Life, Death and Hope in an American Prison* and *Letters to the Sons of Society: A Father's Invitation to Love, Honesty and Freedom*

Introduction

"When I read what I wrote, I felt like I was seeing myself for the
first time! I felt the growth. Writing my story down and sharing
it with others reminds me of this."

— Antwon (Contributor, *When You Hear Me (You Hear Us)*)

This book is the result of nearly 20 years of community building using the life-changing tools of reading and writing. Free Minds was founded in 2002 to fulfill the vision of Glen McGinnis, a young man who discovered his love for reading while on death row in Texas for a crime committed when he was 17 years old. Since his execution, Free Minds has connected with over 1,500 incarcerated and formerly incarcerated youths and adults through book clubs and writing workshops at the DC Jail and juvenile detention center, as well as a correspondence-based book club with DC residents incarcerated in federal prisons across the country, and a reentry book club and peer support program with members who have returned home. Our members are changemakers and peacebuilders. They use their lived experiences and poetry to lead reading, writing, and reflecting sessions with youth and diverse audiences as part of our community-based racial justice education project, On the Same Page.

But it all begins with opening a book and picking up a pen. Many of our members read their first book or write their first poem with Free Minds. Many of them—like Antwon—discover themselves in the process. As Luis shares on page 107, they find hope and process emotions through writing: "Even though there was no love in my life, creating love poems gave me the inspiration to write, to dream, to live. It gave me something to hang on to." We are thrilled to share their powerful, evocative work with you in these pages.

We uplift and center the voices of those directly impacted by the criminal legal system. Building upon our previous two collections, *They Called Me 299-359* and *The Untold Story of the Real Me*, we wanted to broaden the scope and demonstrate the wide-ranging impact of mass incarceration in the US—not only on the young people ensnared in it, but on the community at large, the mothers, the loved ones, the correctional staff, public defenders, prosecutors, and all those who have also been harmed by their proximity to the system and left with unhealed trauma. All of the poets and the majority of those interviewed here have experienced incarceration. But as the stories testify, the prison system does not only affect those who are incarcerated. We are all affected in some way, whether we have known someone who has been incarcerated, we have worked in the system, we have struggled to heal from harm, or we simply live in this society. The prison system has built walls in all of our imaginations, limiting our ideas of what is possible and what we can create together. With *When You Hear Me (You Hear Us)* we hope to reflect the collective impact of the prison system, and our collective responsibility to create a society where every one of us can thrive.

The stories of nearly 100 Free Minds members are represented in this book through their original poetry and through first-person interviews conducted by Free Minds staff and partners. But behind those members stand hundreds more—inside and out—who have worked together since 2002 to create the powerful artistic community that is Free Minds.

These poems were written and interviews were conducted between 2015 and 2021, a period of immense upheaval, of tragedy, struggle, and reckoning—and also of resilience, hope, and creation. The authors in this collection share their own experiences and perspectives, in their own words, with the interviews edited and condensed for publication. While these do not necessarily reflect the views of our organization, we are dedicated to presenting an accurate and diverse reflection of viewpoints and voices to spark dialogue and discussion.

In Free Minds' book clubs, both inside and outside of correctional facilities, we do not always agree with each other, or with the authors of the works we are discussing. But we hold similar goals and values; we always aim to understand each other and the work, and to treat each other with dignity, respect, and compassion. We invite you to do the same with *When You Hear Me (You Hear Us)*. The criminal legal system makes little to no room for freedom of expression and sharing of innovative ideas for change. We believe this is critical for transformative visioning and for imagining a process that acknowledges harm and creates a pathway to healing. We hope the experiences shared on these pages will bring more healing, more creative visioning, more humanity, and above all else, more hope.

Free Minds member Alex, author of "America the Beautiful," described this book as one that "brings different voices together into one collection as if to turn a cacophony into a harmonious symphony."

Thank you for listening to our symphony—and for joining us as we all gather on the same page.

— Free Minds Book Club & Writing Workshop

Why I Write

by John

I write because you cannot turn up your radio to tune me out.

I write because the end is near, and the pen transcends doubt.

I call it quiet noise.

I call it egoism, mixed in with a little confusion and poise.

I fall into a hero system supported by women and small boys that are stalled in a senile realism, living as hard as they can, only to become void.

Most of the time righteousness quickly fades to black, and then there's no one to call it back.

That analytically states we're doomed, to be exact.

That's why I write.

I write because I have to say this one more time.

I write because sometimes things just be on my mind.

I write relief from the stress while I'm doing this grind.

I write because, All Praise Belongs to God, I have to keep trying, hoping my pen leaves something good behind, that's why I write all the time.

I write because I got to, who else gonna do it?

I write because I wanna share with y'all that life is fair, even though we all done been through it.

And I know some don't agree, seeing as how they've been through so much before, so I write to let folks know that it's painful sometimes to love and at the end perhaps it's best to just let go.

I write strong hugs of life, delivering a crippling blow to death.

Barely passing each test, when there's not much life left.

And there's so much life theft, and a major portion of society has digressed into a culture of immediacy, all the while claiming to be doing their best.

I write talent shows for those on the street, and just suppose we help our
    brethren out with food, clothes, and other valuables, who know how they
    may turn out.

I write tears burning out of the strongest mother's eyes on the weakest
    sunny day. How her baby got killed in vain? Why they had to do her baby
    that way?

I write emotions.
I write things down at the slightest notion.
Just to put a thought into quotes... and...

I write from the past first.
I take from those who have already done it right because with life you can't
    rehearse.
Understand my reification, I write because ignorance hurts.

I write because have you ever seen the power of words perfected in a verse?
Because while we read it the crooked lines said it first.
Imagine the first line ever written, priceless it's net worth.
I wrote it, before I quoted it; I cogitated it first.

Words are not harmless magic, I don't just write, I immerse.
And I really contemplate at nights, what's worse?

Being left alone with an empty mind.
Being left alone with empty time.
Being left alone with no peace to find.
That's why I write all the time.

DEAR AMERICA

(JUSTICE)

This chapter features reflections on the American experience today by those who have not shared in its promise. Incarcerated and formerly incarcerated people alongside the child of an incarcerated adult write letters to America, in poetry and prose. Their work illustrates the origins and impact of violence and structural racism, and the lack of accountability that prevents justice. They speak on police violence, the limits of their freedom, and how their exclusion harms the entire society.

America the Beautiful
by Alex

America, today is another glorious day,
the cloudless skies shine bright up there,
helping us feel we'll be alright, for one more night,
as the sun keeps storms away.

America, one of your children went to jail today,
forced to get by without a job,
living hungry with no food to feed his boys,
giving in to doing the only thing he knows,
no matter what it costs.

America, a woman screamed today
claiming a man was threatening her way
though the only evidence she had
was the color of his skin
and the things she planned to say.

America, I am saying this today
because I know you are America the Beautiful
from sea to shining sea,
Land of the Free and Home of the Brave,
where we hold truths to be self-evident
that all men are created equal,
that we are one nation, indivisible,
with liberty and justice for all.

So America please tell me,
what do you have to say?

Lady Liberty

by Miguel

Lady Liberty must be sleep
Or maybe she turned her back
Lady Liberty must be sleep
Or maybe she doesn't care
Lady Liberty must be sleep
Or maybe she's in on it too
Lady Liberty must be sleep
Because there's millions of people in a cage
Lady Liberty must be sleep
Because innocents are dying everyday
Lady Liberty must be sleep
Because those guilty remain free
Lady Liberty must be sleep
Or maybe she's racist too
Lady Liberty must be sleep
Or maybe she just can't see
Lady Liberty must be sleep
Or maybe she's just a disguise
Lady Liberty must be sleep
Because we're still waiting for justice
Lady Liberty must be sleep
Because we're focused on the wrong things
Lady Liberty must be sleep
Because no one follows her values
Lady Liberty must be sleep

Trayvon, Tamir, Michael, Eric, Breonna, etc.
The list is long, now Ahmaud and George

May you rest in peace
With Lady Liberty

Dear America

by Immanuel

Note: This poem was written in 2017.

I'm writing you today, a lost voice from prison
Lost and confused about this country we live in
And the people that's in it
How do you claim to be united, when there's so much division
So much division based on religion
Based on our culture, our sex, and our pigment
Oh, America, how could you be so selfish and ignorant?
To allow a man of this nature, guide us with ignorance
On a path to destruction, I pray for deliverance
For the colored, for the poor, for the Muslim, and immigrant
Oh, America, Oh, America, you have shown your colors
How many years in your country will my people suffer?
I shed tears for my brothers, my sisters, and mothers
The words that you utter have exploited your cover
You, America, have proven racism still exists
The leaders of your nation consist of white supremacists
There are those who follow them and those who are against
A war within your people, your country's at risk
I fear for you, America, but I pray that I am wrong
Sincerely, yours truly, Immanuel

Tony shares his perspective as a child of a parent who was incarcerated for much of his life growing up and to this day.

Tony
(conversation)

At the time of my birth in 1980, my block had become the epicenter of the cocaine trade in Washington, DC. The first open-air drug market for cocaine. I come from Hanover Place—northwest. Cornell Jones, who was one of the biggest drug kingpins in the history of the city—he's a Hanover guy. He was my dad's mentor, if you will. And when federal and local authorities what we call "shut down Hanover" in '85, Cornell Jones goes to prison and my father kind of assumes his position. And around '86, '87 is when him and Rayful Edmond, they start doing business together.

At the time, obviously, I didn't understand my dad's a major drug dealer. That's the only world I knew. So nothing is abnormal in my mind. But I know he doesn't have a job. And I know that people treat us different from everybody else—especially in our neighborhood, but even at restaurants or the barbershop or stores. You know, we had our own parking space at the Capital Centre.[1] And every other man that I know, right, this is his lifestyle, as well. I didn't really know people who worked, particularly men.

In '89, I distinctly remember we were home and we're beeping him—you know, pagers—and he's not calling back. I don't understand what's going on. But I could just sense this, like, anxiety. And just this look in everybody's eyes, the adults, like deer in the headlights. Nobody knows what's going on. And then it gets confirmed because it comes on TV—"City

---

1   The Capital Centre was a sports arena in DC used for NBA and NHL games.

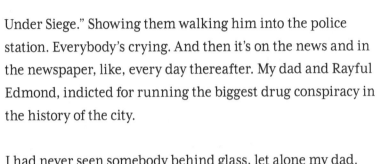

Under Siege." Showing them walking him into the police station. Everybody's crying. And then it's on the news and in the newspaper, like, every day thereafter. My dad and Rayful Edmond, indicted for running the biggest drug conspiracy in the history of the city.

I had never seen somebody behind glass, let alone my dad. They were high-profile prisoners, so they had to go into these cages. I mean, even though they're behind the glass, they got to go in a cage. They're fully shackled. And talking on the phone through the glass like that as a 9-year-old ... it killed me. Particularly when you had to leave. I would cry for hours as soon as the visit was over. All the way home. You know, I love my father. That's my superhero. That was extremely traumatic. But I would still want to go see him. Tuesdays and Fridays—I'll never forget it. My mother would drive me. But she wouldn't come in. I would go in with his girlfriend. So just imagine all that tension.

When I think back to the conversations when he first went to jail. He's 26. He doesn't know what to say to me. Nobody does. He received life without the possibility of parole. And I remember, we went to see him at Quantico. You know, he's in his cell. He crying. I never saw him cry. He's trying to wipe his tears away. And he's just telling me I got to be strong and all of this stuff. I'll never forget that. That's, like, burned into my memory. But I can see the fear. Just the fear. Not only about what he was about to face—life without parole, right? But more, like, what's going to happen to me?

The stress of all that, the trauma, really took my mom's sanity. And so my mother started to battle schizophrenia and depression. That was the most significant loss. For me. And

challenge. Watching her go through that and deteriorate. How many mothers across this country are left to pick the pieces up, right? Or grandmothers. The first time my mom went to St. Elizabeths,[2] I was 14. She went through my teenage years—when I was 15, when I was 17. But even when she didn't get committed, at home it was a lot to deal with. You kind of become the person taking care of that person, you know? Thank god for my grandmother.

It was way too much going on in my community and in my family. Through the 90's, Washington, DC is the murder capital of the United States. Hanover is still a major drug market. It became increasingly violent in my teenage years. My mother at St. Elizabeths. My father doing life in prison. People shooting at us every day. It was super tough. I don't know, really, how I did it. What they instilled in me early really carried me, though.

Education was always important in my household. So I just wanted to make them proud, even if they weren't there with me like before. I think that's what continued to kind of push me. And from ninth grade to 12th grade, I went to Gonzaga.[3] Oh, my god [laughs] it was just so different from anything that I had ever experienced. Just complete culture shock. I remember the first time a person asked me, "Where did you summer?" I was, like, *What the... In Hanover.* I think the assumption was that I was just like everybody else. But I was just, like, every day, just make it to 2:30 and go back to my world. Which was literally just stepping across K Street.

---

2   St. Elizabeths is a psychiatric hospital in Washington, DC.

3   Gonzaga College High School is a private college-preparatory high school in Washington, DC. The majority of the students are white.

First 13 years in prison, my father was in Lompoc, California. So basically, from age nine until I was 22, he was 3,000 miles away, on the other side of the country. I went out [to visit him] three times. When I was 12, when I was 16, and then when I was 19. At 12, by that time, he had got married to the girlfriend. What I distinctly remember about that is seeing him be affectionate with her. But I never saw him kiss my mother or be affectionate towards my mother. That angered me. My parents would fight a lot too when I was younger—and I was old enough to kind of be, like, you used to hit my mother, bro. So all of those things were going on inside of me. You know what I'm saying? I remember that visit being marked by those feelings. But also, at the same time, I hadn't seen him in two and a half years. Right? So I'm also excited.

By 16, my mother had kind of descended totally. To me, I'm, like, a man myself. So I'm trying to catch him up, trying to talk to him. He's been in a penitentiary for this time. So he's changed too. He's more hardened, you know? And I can see that. Like, everything is just rigid with him. Like, "Listen, this is what you do." His main thing was always, *Stay out of trouble. Don't do this. Don't do that. Do that.* And like, that's cool, I hear that. But how do I do that? I ain't the 9-year-old boy no more, and I still live there. And my friends getting killed, bro. But you don't even know my friends. At that point, I wouldn't challenge anything that he said, I would just be, like, "Cool, okay." But I knew in my mind, when I go back, I got to do what I got to do. Like, you're not there.

At 19, I'm out of high school. I'm an adult. At that point, it's like, what I'm going to do in life and taking a stand and remaining safe, not getting in trouble, not getting in the street. But also just talking about all the challenges of what's going on in the city and in my neighborhood. All that I've lost by that point, you know. And just hoping and praying that he could, at some point, come home. On jail visits—it's like a first date, kind of, you know? Even though you know the person. You're not trying to come on a visit and give all bad news. Like, they're already in a bad situation. You know what I'm saying? Like, for real. Early on, I figured something out: that he couldn't do anything about it. So why give him extra stress? Why? He can't do anything about it anyway. Whatever's going on out here, I have to deal with it.

It was rough, but I knew people loved me. And so many of my homies, they didn't have that. I got friends who didn't even go to sixth grade. Had to just start taking care of themselves at 11. Mother on crack. Father never was around anyway. I mean, nothing in the refrigerator. That kind of thing. And I think that stopped me from sulking.

My uncles would win some money or rob a bank—and I ain't justifying that behavior. But that stuff would allow me some cushion. And our lights were always on. Our heat was always on. You know, I didn't have the lifestyle that I had once had. But I had something. My friends, a lot of them, they had to go out there and get it. And I saw what that level of desperation did to their decision-making ability or decisions they felt like they had to make to survive. It wasn't necessarily decisions they wanted to make. And, I mean, as boys, not even young men. Literally. Boys. Not even to mention things that may have happened to them in their households that I don't even know. You understand? Based on that lack of stability and protection and guidance from adults. And so I was just really blessed. Very lucky. The fate of most of my friends, the guys I was with every day, was jailed or they died. Just the reality of my

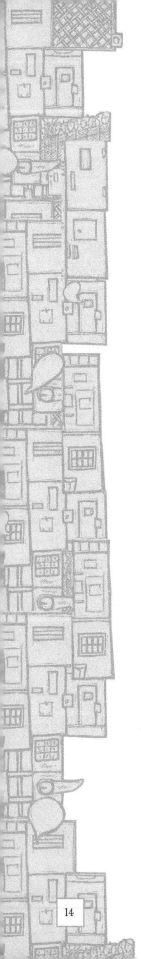

generation in the city. It was, like, death or prison.

My father was sent to FCI Cumberland in Maryland when I was 22. Two hours away. So close, but still so far away. I have two daughters now—and I want them to have a relationship with my father. But I really hate taking them. Oh, my god, it's hard. I never wanted that for my children. Last time we went, when we were leaving—he has to go back through a door and we go to exit. And my daughter asked—and she was kind of loud, like the other incarcerated people, they heard what she said—"Pop-Pop, why you got to go back there? Why can't you just come with us?" You know, it was deep. He had to kind of compose himself. He said, "This is where I got to go." And I was praying, like, *I hope she doesn't ask me...* You know, she doesn't know yet that that's jail. But she has an understanding that jail is a place that you don't want to go—even cartoons or whatever talk about bad guys in jail and I've heard her make comments about that. So, it becomes something that I, even now as an adult, have to deal with as a result of his incarceration. This generational trauma you're passing down.

Gone in Body, Spirit Never to Be Forgotten

by Saulina

They try to make you think, you have died in silence

But your blood cries out to the Most High God

A body taken, never to grow old, but

A soul awakened, never to grow cold

Who are they to tell you your place is beneath them

Because your skin and philosophies can compete with theirs

Is it really the statues you worry about?

Is it really the history you're trying to preserve?

You'd be lying if you answered yes

For we all know, once those statues start coming down

You will be so afraid too many of us will rise up

So quick to change the outcome of the war

The war your forefathers fought against

Praising an army who conspired in his very home

In his very bedroom, stealing his life and presidency

See, unlike you, we honor who fall in righteousness

Unlike you, we celebrate the freedom the Union brought

So you can keep killing the body

Because one day, God is going to show you

It is YOUR spirit that will soon be FORGOTTEN

Quintessence of African American

by Phillip

My country...
'Tis of thee.
Bittersweet land, apparition of liberty.
So long withheld from me...

Of thee I see
Land where my fathers died,
Land where the pilgrims cried.
A pretense of courtesy,
But held disdain deep.
Likewise, today people in positions of authority
And opportunity.

My country...
When will you unchain the shackles: mentally,
Historically, and physically
That bind us
Civilly to hypocrisy.

Labels

by Jameon

I am the black label
    And I ain't talking no polo
Even though the PO-AIM-LOW
    Turning black lives into matter
But when did altered material matter?
    Above what actually matters?
        I guess only
Red, white, and blue is the true-life that really matters
    As a matter of fact
Born at Children's Hospital, 1982
    My inheritance is the self-endearment of being a n*gga!
Etched in the minds of Confederates
    But the arousing excitement of this ignorance
Is equal bliss
    Invisible inside a nation that's indivisible!
I had no choice but to become a victim
    Within my blood-flowing, poverty-stricken come-unity
To some victimizer
    In sincere search of a victimless crime
Justice being accursed blind
    Caused many monumental inequalities!
Especially to an offense worse than treason
    Walking while being labeled black
Is enough reason
    For me to lose my life this evening

Who Says?

by Antonio L.

Who says I can't be what I want to be?
'Cause I grew up in the average black society
And tried to be, more than what you said I could
After the fact that you lied to me

Deprived me of my dreams that were written far within my reach
Afraid I would find out the truth
So, is that why you lie when you teach?

Come on, you can do better than that
Is it because I'm black that makes me a threat?

D*mn, then why are you so upset
At the fact that I achieved far more than you could believe
In a nation where blacks are considered failures?
So, is that why you deceive?

Charles, Chris, Cliff, Kelvin, Levy, Tim
(conversation)

Eight young men were tried in the 1984 murder of Catherine Fuller in a Northeast Washington, DC alley. Only one of them had ever been arrested before. Despite the lack of any physical evidence, all were convicted and sentenced to life in prison. The men were among 17 young people rounded up in the weeks after the murder and purported to be part of the "8th and H Street Crew," a group that people in the neighborhood insist never existed. The youngest, Cliff, was 16 at the time of the crime. Cliff was interrogated for 19 hours without his mother or an attorney present. Ultimately, he made a video confession which he later said was coerced by detectives who stuck his head inside a toilet and beat him so badly he had to be taken to the hospital. Cliff says he relented when detectives promised him he could go home to his mother if he repeated their story. All of the men have maintained their innocence over more than three decades. One died in prison. One remains incarcerated. Six of them have been released on parole after spending the bulk of their adult lives in prison.

KELVIN: We watched the homicide detectives go through the neighborhood questioning a lot of guys and coming up in their houses and all that. I came home one Sunday and my grandma said, "The police were just looking for you!" I turned on the news, and I seen Christopher, Russell, and all them getting locked up and they said they was looking for more and I said, "Oh no! I *know* they ain't trying to put this on us!"

CHARLES: When you get locked up for something that you didn't do, even if they ask you about it or accuse you of it, well,

you know you didn't do it! And they speak to you as if they gonna make sure the right thing happen, so it puts you at ease. If you didn't have anything to do with it, you gonna be let free. You alright. And you believe these people are gonna make sure that the right thing happens.

TIM: I was 19 years old. When the police was making their little rounds they stopped at my house twice. They told me, "We know you didn't have anything to do with it, but we know you know a lot of people." I didn't know nothing to tell them nothing. A few weeks later, it's seven in the morning, I'm upstairs with the family. We hear a bunch of police banging at the door. I look over at Russell, and he said, "I ain't did nothing," and I said, "I ain't did nothing!" I never seen so many guns in my life. They slam me on the floor. My aunt's asking, "What you doing with my baby?" They was like, "We locking him up for murder!" I'm down on the floor, looking up at them like, "Murder?"

KELVIN: The murder was serious. This was the mother of someone we grew up with. Mrs. Fuller had babysat a lot of us guys on this case. It was so sad what happened to her. But never in my mind, did I think I would be convicted of this crime. We thought the police would do the right thing. One of those detectives hung in our neighborhood. A lot of those officers played basketball with us at the rec center and all that. This detective *knew* this wasn't in our character. There wasn't any ifs ands or buts, he knew this wasn't in our character. But he didn't speak up about it. He went along with the people falsely accusing us for this crime. It's hard for me to trust in the law anymore. I just kept saying, "This lie isn't gonna hold up." But the lie did hold up.

TIM: When they got me to the police station, it done flipped all the way around. Now they want me to sign a paper saying I would testify on Levy. They told me, "Jump off the train before it take off. You don't want to be with the rest of them." I said, "I'm not signing no paper!" Eventually they tell me, "Either you gonna sign this paper saying you gonna testify, or we gonna put you in it and make sure you get 35 years out of it!" And that was the only truth I know about this case. I ended up with 35 years to life.

CLIFF: I had just graduated out of junior high school. I was 16 years old. I didn't really know who I was. I just knew my name. At 16 years old, I knew I was Clifton. This my parents, them was my friends. I just knew my name. I never been in this situation before.

CHARLES: They went to Cliff for a reason. It's not no accident. Everything was calculated.

KELVIN: When it came to this case, they played by their own rules and they didn't care what it took. Cliff was a child. There's no way he 'sposed to be interrogated for all that time without his parents or an attorney there. It's like they planned to get him to do what they wanted him to do. They misled him to believe he was going to go home if he would say the things they wanted him to say.

TIM: He was the fish! The easy prey. The only thing Cliff understood was that he wanted to go home. It was easier for them to manipulate him.

CLIFF: It was a brutal interrogation. They put my head in the toilet. Instead of repeating their statement, I should've just let them beat me. Ay, if you take my life, you do. Them blowing smoke and telling me lies. Like, "Your mother's in the lobby, she's waiting for you." But she wasn't. I thought doing what they told me to do, I would go home. But it wasn't that way.

TIM: When they announced that guilty verdict, my life never been rocked like that. To this day, my life never been rocked like that. It's something I hope nobody else ever has to experience. When you ain't done nothing. And you *know* you ain't done it. And they're about to send you away for a long time.

CHARLES: My brother Chrissy started crying. He was one of the toughest dudes I ever knew. To see him cry, it was crazy. You wonder, *Is this real?* You know it's real. You've just been convicted and it's bad!

KELVIN: It was unbelievable. My life was over.

LEVY: I thought I'd never see my family again.

CLIFF: I didn't understand anything in the courtroom. When we got convicted, I still thought I would be able to go home afterwards.

CHRIS: All police did not do this to us. A group of individuals who acted outside of the law did this to us. They manipulated, mistreated and abused us, to get a group of young people off the street when they had a case that needed to be solved. We all suffered a great injustice. This was the most publicized case in the history of Washington, DC, ever. It affected families. It affected us as individuals. It divided our entire community. There was no middle ground. You had to pick and choose sides. And that was so unfair to the community when they

never had all the facts. The people who didn't get justice in the end are the Fuller family and all of us who were falsely convicted.

CHARLES: You have to turn a switch when you go to prison. When I went to prison, my train of thought just changed over. I knew I was there under false pretenses and I knew at some point I would be in a position where I'd have to defend that. I'm sure all of us went through that.

KELVIN: Going to prison, we all heard the rumors. They said people were going to kill us when we got there because of the case. But we all knew we didn't do it, and we were standing on that principle. I was in prison probably about six months before an officer called me the N-word. From there, they sent me to one of the most dangerous prisons in the system. When we all went in, the guys from DC was at war with the Aryan Brotherhood. A race war was going on. Even though we had nothing to do with this war when we came in, we were from DC, so we had to watch our back. Prison can change you. But you can't let it break you. You can't lose yourself inside them walls. I never lost hope and faith that one day I would be home. It took 35 years.

CHRIS: We all went through the same things. We all lost loved ones, lost our parents. We were separated. Some of us never got to correspond or talk to each other for over 20 years. But nobody understands what we been through but us. It bonded us. It became a glue. It gave us an impregnable friendship that can never be broken.

CHARLES: We all *still* suffer the same things. You have to deal with people out here who wonder if you did it. You tell them your name and they find out who you are and a stigma is placed on us. It's on all of us.

LEVY: They're always gonna say, "That's the guy!" "He one of them!" "That's one of the 8th and H guys." It goes on and on, people still label us. It's never going to stop.

KELVIN: I couldn't cry in prison. You go into prison with your emotions, but in prison, emotions get people killed. That first night after I was released, I sat alone in my room. It was the first time that I shed a tear. I shed a tear for that conviction. I shed a tear for when I lost my 20-year-old daughter who died when I was in prison. I shed a tear for when I lost my mother. I just took a deep breath and I let it all out.

CHARLES: Society will never understand, regardless if we ever get recognized as innocent. Nobody will never understand what we have been through. They'll never understand that they stole our whole young adulthood. A lot of the people that I ran with when we were kids, are now happily married, hardworking tax-paying citizens. I wonder what I would have been able to do? Where would I be now?

CLIFF: There is one thing that bothered me then, 37 years ago, and it bothers me now. I always wonder how my co-defendants all felt about what took place for me in the interrogation room. They all encourage me not to let it bother me. They say they understand the position they had me in. But it still bother me. I feel like I hurt them and that hurts me.

KELVIN: We always tell Clifton, don't worry about feeling this way, or that you hurt us. That video tape was a product of what the system did to you. We knew it was a lie. He's our brother.

He's family and we love him.

TIM: We been in this long haul together. What's done is done. Cliff went down with us.

CHRIS: No matter what, we are all together. This only drew us closer.

KELVIN: We just look forward to enjoying the rest of our lives. Spending time with loved ones, giving back and speaking out. One day a week, we make sure we get together. We go bowling, go out to eat, cook out, hang out and play pool. We cut jokes and have fun. That's our time to spend together and talk about whatever is bothering the next guy. Because nobody can understand our pain but us.

CLIFF: I was hurt by what the detectives did to us. But I don't feel bitter. Me and my brothers know the truth.

CHRIS: We don't have bitterness in our hearts. Now, don't misunderstand, we're not happy about what was done to us, but we don't harbor bitterness. Because if you do, then you're still in prison and they win.

CHARLES: I don't have time to be mad at everyone in the world. There are so many things I want to experience. I don't think about jail. I'm out here now and jail is behind me. I am too in love with the world to be mad or angry.

LEVY: In my heart, I believe the truth gonna come out. That pushes me to go forward and keep moving. I'm not looking back. Regardless of what anybody say, I know the truth. So, I'm good.

CHRIS: We can take the high road. We can take this experience and move on and give back to our community. It's a testimony of our strength, of our character. That's our way of proving them wrong.

After several witnesses recanted their testimony, saying that it was coerced by police, it was also determined that the government had withheld evidence they should have shared with the defense. Prosecutors knew, but did not disclose, that several witnesses reported seeing a man at the scene of the crime who had committed several other attacks and robberies of women in the neighborhood. In 2017, the Supreme Court turned down the convicted men's appeal for a new trial. The Mid-Atlantic Innocence Project continues its work to exonerate them.

Charles came home in June of 2020 after 36 years behind bars. He works full-time as a maintenance technician and still manages to run several miles every day in his Capitol Hill neighborhood. He also volunteers on weekends passing out food to people experiencing homelessness—something his grandmother taught him to do at a young age. Charles looks forward to one day owning his own home.

Chris served almost 26 years in prison. He was given the most lenient sentence because he was a high school graduate. He is a supervisor for a parking lot company. He is passionate about working in and for the community, serving youth, seniors, people who are homeless, and formerly incarcerated people.

Cliff served more than 34 years in prison. He came home in March 2019. He enjoys spending time with his family, and works as a parking valet. He regularly speaks to middle school, high school, and college students across the city as a Free Minds Poet Ambassador. Cliff plans to open a Boys & Girls Club one day with a big gymnasium and a recording studio to lift up DC youth.

Kelvin was released in October 2019 after serving 35 years in prison. He is a glazier apprentice working on installing windows in large commercial buildings. He is enjoying traveling around the country and his newest hobby, bowling. Most of all, he loves spending time with his two daughters. His goal is to open his own concrete floor polishing business.

Levy was released in January 2020 after serving 36 years in prison. He works as a supervisor with a janitorial maintenance services company that hires and trains returning citizens to enter the workforce. His dream is to get married and have a family. Levy loves providing outreach to youth in the community. He sees it as a way to spread hope.

Tim spent nearly 36 years in prison before being released in November 2020. He loves working in the kitchen and hopes to land a job in a restaurant. Until then, he works full time as a laborer in a brickyard. He loves the little things about freedom—like going for a drive and watching the beautiful scenery go by.

Hidden Within the 13th

by Kendricus

One word killed the Eric Garners and George Floyds of America.

One word deprived them of life and happiness.

One word hinders African Americans from the sweet joy of liberty.

One word denies us our equality.

One word allows injustices to go unchecked.

One word permits the violation of our rights.

One word created mass incarceration.

One word killed the Sandra Blands and Breonna Taylors of America.

One word will keep black lives inferior.

One word.

The word... **"except."**

Amendment XIII

Slavery Abolished

[Proposed by Congress Jan. 31 1865, ratified Dec. 6 1865]

Section 1. Neither slavery nor involuntary servitude, **except** as a punishment for crime whereof the party shall have been duly convicted, shall exist within the United States, or any place subject to their jurisdiction.

"I will never forget what a great shock this was to me, here, for the first time, I was made aware of the existence of a race problem."

— Dr. Martin Luther King Jr. [1929-1968]

8:46[1]

by Gene

8 minutes and 46 seconds, handcuffed and no weapon
Your fellow officer not helping
Instead, opts for looking out, while onlookers record
The death of George Floyd

Pleas for his life were null and void
Another Black life destroyed
By the hands of those sworn to protect us, but how can we be protected
When we're constantly suspected, based on our complexion
And perpetually subjected to social injustice
Hundreds of years of oppression, yet we keep stepping
Just to get them thrown back by 8 minutes and 46 seconds

That knee is heavy! I can't BREATHE!
No! I can't believe that 2020 and 1920 have so much in common
From mass incarceration, to unmasking racism, it's alarming!
But they ostracized Colin for taking a knee, at least his was for peace
And not to cut off air supply of a helpless guy

Resisting arrest? No! Resisting his death!
But when viewed as a threat it's a safe bet that you won't get
Treated with respect
Now the world in protest and unrest
Because your blatant murder and disregard for Black lives is unjust
Change? We won't get change or progress until there's a change in the
White House and Congress

---

1   In 2020, Minneapolis police officer Derek Chauvin knelt on George Floyd's neck for nine minutes
     and twenty-nine seconds. This was originally reported as eight minutes and forty-six seconds,
     with 8:46 becoming a protest symbol.

Not just another political promise, but sufficient action
Because your current system shows that Black Lives Don't Matter

8 minutes and 46 seconds it took me to write this poem
Rest in Peace George Floyd, I wrote this for him

Words Can't Explain

by Jamal

She didn't deserve the way the police

Came and gunned 'em down

Tears running down her pretty face

'Cause she lost her child

Now she mourns for the times he'll never be around

Rayvon, Trayvon, Lil Kenny, Black Mills

It's the moments we dread like this

Tryna make it in this world

They saying don't fit

Black hands in the sky balled in a fist

Black lives hold it down

So we represent

Look how far we came

Our Value
by Arthur

What is the value of Blk life?

About $20

During slavery, a Blk male was valued

At about $100

In the criminal justice system

A Blk male is worth

$40,000 a year

While free, in society, his value

Is but $20

Just ask George Floyd

THE WAR
THAT REPLAYS
IN MY MIND

(GROWING UP)

Here, writers reflect on some of the factors contributing to incarceration, and a former public defender speaks to the toll incarceration takes on all those involved. Poverty, drugs, death, and struggle create a climate of conflict and volatility, exacerbated by the lack of supportive infrastructure that stretches from lost family to laws that leave children vulnerable. Systemic neglect and harm has a lasting impact on these writers' neighborhoods.

Against These Odds

by Antonio C.

Against all odds
All these odds against black men in DC
These shoes I have on my feet
Have to jump so many hurdles in a race to be free
If I do well in school
Can I jump over jail?
If I pray every night
Can I jump over hell?
If I run past time
Will time really tell?
Or will my shoes turn into boots
As I write this next poem from a cell?
Will the preachers say a special prayer?
Do the social workers really care?
It's hard because I'm so young
It shouldn't be my fault
These shoes had to jump so many hurdles
Before I could even walk
As I look out the window
And I see dope fiends nod
I just say, I'm a young brother
Against all these odds

War Child

by Nick

Inspired by War Child: A Child Soldier's Story *by Emmanuel Jal*

Oh War Child,
look at what you have become
oppressed by a system that forced you to become wild
in the merge of guns and a mind that has no conscience
you have become a war child
seeing blood flow from out the flesh of another has no case in your file
it's just another memory that been shot
Pow!!!!

Oh War Child
yes, you, African boy
you've been dredged from the hands of your sweet mother
and now look at you
angry by the fault of your circumstances
so you have no care in this world because you feel that you are on your own
but you are not alone
yes I feel the pain that trickles my soul
the war that replays in my mind is long lasting, it never seems to get old
watching the bloodbath of my brothers drown them to death has triggered me
to become cold

Oh War Child
look at what I have become
guns were my expression of the G-Code
and the fault of me being away from my sweet mother
has put me in depression of the survivor mode
frustration has ruled my thoughts

all my effort to find a way out had seem to led to naught
there was no place for freedom
I was caught up in the system of oppression but

Oh War Child
you are not alone
I too am looking to find a way out

Counting

by Alisha

I counted three liquor stores on my block

Over sixty black men and four police cars

Counting

I'm counting...

Seven people in my mother's home, two bedrooms, and one stove

One bathroom, nineteen weed roaches in the ashtray

Six dollars on her bedroom dresser and two bags under her eyes

I'm counting

Still counting...

72 hours alone, four calls from our school, and only one box of cereal left

Four eyes on me, four eyes looking through a shoe box

15 years and one judge

I'm counting

Still counting...

3 brothers left, one welfare card, zero phone calls

Three different states, too many lies

And I promise, I know how to count because I'm nine now

I'm counting four therapists, two psychiatrists, thirty days, eight needles, and
    one wish

I'm counting one mother, two brothers, and no fire alarm

Seven tubes, no tears, and every, "I hate you," I ever spoke

I'm counting...

Three men, no voice, every threat

Fifteen, eight prior charges, one baby

Two lives, one hundred and twenty-two cells, but no help

I'm counting

Still counting...

Hosea
(conversation)

My mother had a dream. She was going to Howard University when she met my dad. But then my mom got pregnant. She had to drop out of school and ended up having another baby right after the first. All of a sudden, instead of a student going after her dream, she just had all of these kids. When I was two years old, she had a mental breakdown. That was in 1994. She not dead or nothing. She just fled.

By that time, my father, he was running the streets and getting incarcerated. Child Protective Services came in and got all of the kids. They split us up. Me and my older sister ended up with our aunt. She took care of us, but she and everyone else made sure we knew that she wasn't our mom. We didn't have a mom.

It used to make me sad when I'd see other little kids with their mothers. I'd see the kids crying, *Mommy! Mommy!* And I knew I couldn't run to anybody and say *Mommy! Mommy!* You know what I'm saying? So it was like, I ain't never get that pampering and them hugs and them kisses. I feel like the way you get compassion, and the way you get mercy, is from having a nurturing mother around you constantly showing you these things. I think not having my mother made me more drawn to violence and the street life.

I was probably like 10 years old when I was looking out my window one day and I heard some gunshots. I didn't duck or nothing. Nah, I ran to the window to look! I just see a big

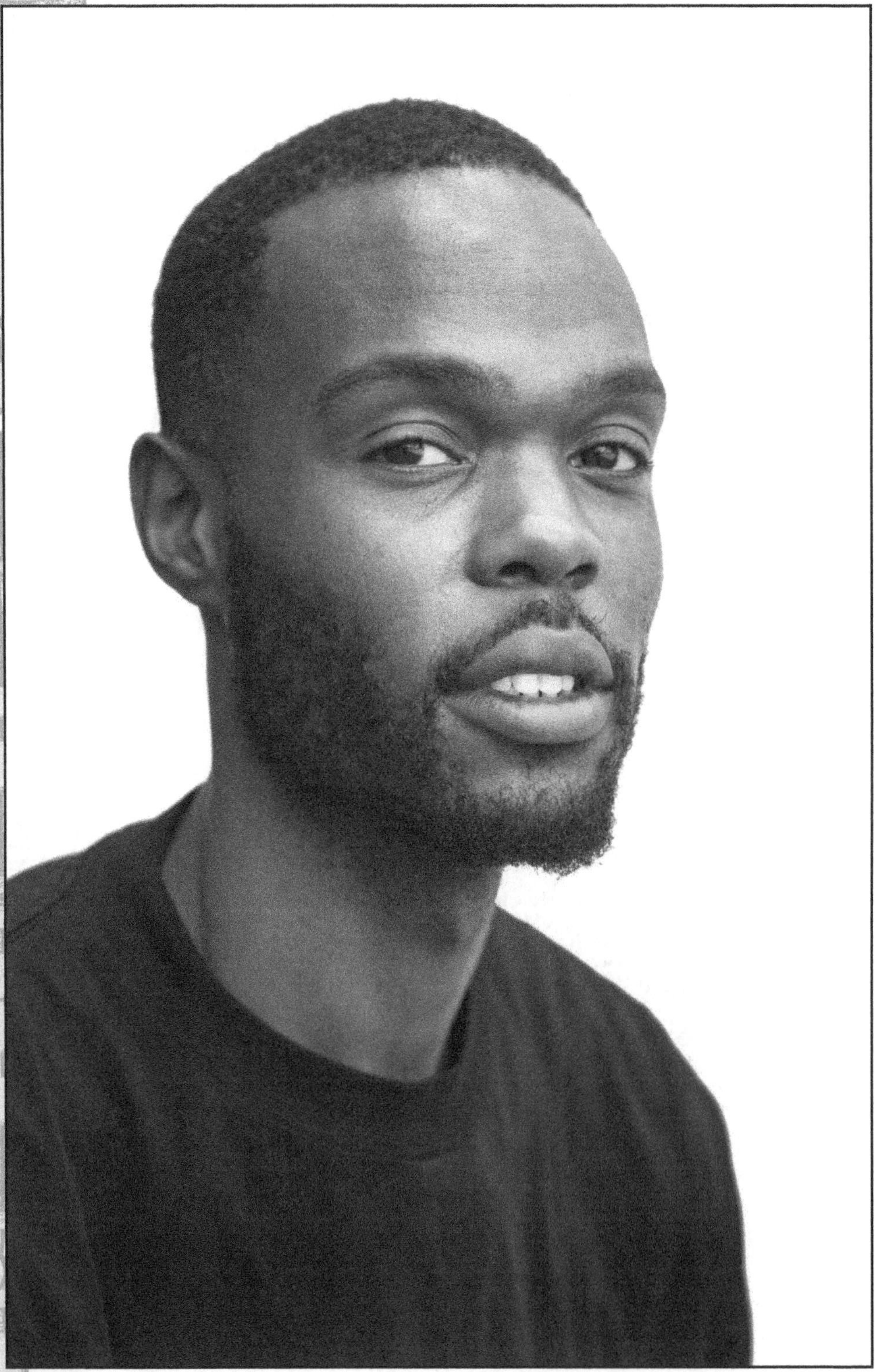

chrome gun in a dude's hand, shooting at another dude. *Boom! Boom! Boom!* I know I should have been afraid, but I was excited! I was like, *Dang!* You know? It was like a movie. I'd heard how the older dudes talked about it, and now I finally seen it in real life!

When I started junior high, we were segregated by neighborhood. We coming in to junior high at 12, and the older kids would say, *Y'all come from around my way, okay, let's clique up together. Y'all around that way, y'all together.* So that's when we started fighting for our neighborhoods. *We from here. You're not.* Next thing you know, we're fighting after school.

From then on, violence and hustling were just a part of life. From where I stood, there really wasn't an alternative option that I could see. And it may sound crazy, but I wasn't looking for anything else. When I stepped on my front porch, I saw people smoking weed, selling drugs, crackheads, dope fiends, you know what I'm saying? In the absence of my mother, all of my role models were men. I wanted to be like my big brothers, my uncles, and even my father. They was drug dealers and gangsters and I saw them getting respect. Everywhere I went with them, somebody knew them. They got a lot of love. That felt good. At the end of the day, I became a product of my environment. I was young and I didn't see nothing else. This is what the people I looked up to were doing. I wanted to be like them and so I chased it.

When I was 17, I could take something from somebody and not even feel bad about it. My conscience just wasn't intact yet. I was arrested for robbery and charged as an adult. I went to prison and had everything taken away from me. I didn't own nothing, had no possessions. All I had was me. I began to

work out, and read books. I grew to value myself more. Now, I'm older and I'm different. I feel so bad for the victims of my crime. Now they feel traumatized and they scared to come out of their house. What I did made life worse for them. I can't take something from nobody now. I grew and matured on my own. I grew a conscience.

Hosea is 29 years old. He was sentenced as an adult at the age of 17. He works as a clerk for the US Postal Service and owns three small businesses: an online travel agency, a body-sculpting service, and an e-commerce fashion company. He has also developed and published a mobile game app. Hosea is the father of two young daughters and says everything he does is for them.

From Birth

by Antonio G.

I guess from the day of birth

My moms knew what I was worth

From the day of birth

I popped out looking ugly and sad

So my moms and pops got mad

And wished they would've put me in a body bag

Or left me in the alleyway

Leaking with a toe tag

From the day of birth

I guess my moms knew

That my ugliness would only get worse

From the day of birth

I cried out for society

To recognize all my pains and hurts

It seems like from the day of birth

I was locked up in a jail cell

Feeling in my heart that I'm going straight to hell

I guess from the day of birth

I knew all my strengths would become nothing but hurt

And that society would be looking down on me with big azz smirks

Dear Lord, that hurts

From the day of birth

Absent Father

by Andre G.

Being struck by a bullet, serious pain repeatedly
broken promises is an excruciating feeling, one in the same.

Touch down, prom flix, memories not shared,
sports to graduations, gave me your word you'd be there.

Something came up, or you caught a flat tire.

Love shielded the real you, forever a habitual liar.

When you die and I don't grieve people, ask me how I cope.

I tell them to thank you for not being there.

Shout out to my "False Hopes."

21 Guns

by Dimitri

Stuck in this world

Where I feel so alone

Froze on face, a cold stare

Like the Arctic was my home

Keep calling on God

But he never answers the phone

Where else am I supposed to turn

When a house is not a home?

Six feet deep

Is the only time I'll sleep

'Cause if you close ya eyes once

Then the devil surely creeps

Black birds on the sill

But they never make a peep

Eager vultures on the watch

Waiting on the lost of feet

Feel my pain

Like aching bones from when it rains

It's a permanent strain

Wish I could get out of this game

Where everyone loses

And the winner becomes insane

I welcome a quick death

21 guns scream bang, bang!

My Block

by DeAngelo J.

They sell rocks
My Block
They tote Glocks
My Block
You hear shots
My Block
A lot of bodies drop
My Block
We need a better spark
My Block
Cameras watch
My Block
It needs to stop

El Salvador

by Ever

Born in a place that got the Creator's name

So beautiful and lovely

Poor, but honorable

The country of corn and mangos

Small, but crowded

Honor to the flag of El Salvador

The thumb of America

Blue and white

My blood is blue

Small, but strong

Violence has overthrown

All of this murder and homicide

Darkened our beautiful flag

Presidents have sworn to take care of the country

But they are more corrupt than all this crime

We have let our nation fall

Fallen, deep nation

That has the Creator's name

Is crying tears of blood

El Salvador, don't worry

'Cuz I won't let you down

I am proud of being born

In the best country

El Salvador

Under Difficult Circumstances

by William

In the circumstances for which I was born

I take the form of a young brotha

Birth by a young motha

No fatha to make whole what was incomplete

July 26 year '92 I was already defeated

But as the years moved on I grew

I didn't want to face the fact that I must taste the end of my demise

Fix your ears and not your eyes and you can still see

How sorrow cries

Feel how solemn my speech is when intertwined with

My lyrical ties

Producing more in my mind when in the state of production

Devising a plan tryna make it to what I think is the end

Trying not to crash with my opposite making a bone breakin' percussion

But it really don't matter cuz it was over once they said begin

I can't win

So I pass the torch and knowledge to my reproduction

Don't leave 'em answers, I leave 'em questions cuz questions lead to answers

When produced under difficult circumstances

Andrew
(conversation)

My first summer of law school I worked with the ACLU in Philadelphia. And my first assignment that first summer was being sent as the ACLU's representative to this meeting of former prisoners who had all served their time at Holmesburg Prison, outside of Philadelphia. It turned out that they had been the subject of human experimentation because pharmaceutical companies and others used them as test subjects, and they had suffered ill health effects.

The ACLU said, *Maybe we should look into suing, let's bring some of the Holmesburg survivors together.* So, I'm just a first-year law student then, but my boss said, "Look, no one's really going to show up to this meeting. Go be the ACLU representative. Tell them what we're thinking about and report back." And so I walk into this room, and there are about 45 men waiting for "their lawyer"—who is me. This meeting that was supposed to take a few minutes took three and a half hours and ended with them taking off their shirts and showing me their physical scars and injuries from the testing. And my world was sort of opened to this horror of what prison did to people. How it was not helping people, and how there were no real legal remedies for these clear harms. Even in this particular case, they couldn't bring a lawsuit because there was no way to show the causation of these particular human experiments and the ultimate medical conditions. So I said, *Well, maybe I'll try to keep people out of prison in the first place,* and so I decided to become a public defender.

I think your role as a public defender is to make sure that no

Andrew shares his perspective as a public defender for many years.

one forgets the human being sitting next to you. Everyone wants to think of your clients as a case number or a crime or a statistic. And your job is to make sure that the judge, the jurors, and the community see them as deep, complex human beings who cannot be forgotten. It is your job to stand with this person who otherwise society would very much like to just lock away, ignore, or warehouse somewhere. And to shake up that system and say, actually, there are these legal and moral principles you have to uphold. Before you act, you have to be convinced beyond a reasonable doubt about a fellow human being, and the doubt runs to the benefit of my client.

Some of defending is storytelling. Some of it is showing why this person deserves another chance. And some of it is finding those things that reveal humanity, including poetry. Poetry represents deep, raw, personal feeling—*This is what I feel about my mother, my street, my experience.* You can actually watch judges get shaken by it. The truth is that judges also see trauma every day. And the only way, I think, that many can really manage that trauma is to sort of close off from that hurt and build walls. And so, when you have something poetic that cracks those walls and says, no, you have to look and read the poetry of my client saying how he was abandoned by his mother and how he's had no one, the walls come down.

A lot of the judges want to find hope in the people before them. This kid may have shot someone, but he's young, he can change, and we have no idea who he will become after the time he has to serve. Judges want defendants to give them hope that they will do something good in this life. Sometimes the voice of poetry is that hope. It shows insight. It shows remorse. It shows some of the traumas going on from growing up in a dangerous world with mental health issues and drug addiction and the violence that is part of growing up in certain areas of DC.

We don't think of ordinary daily violence as trauma, but it is. If it's dangerous for you to walk from your house to your school and you've watched people get shot in front of you, it has to affect how you react. And those daily traumas get compounded by poverty and the concerns of not having enough food to eat. It's horrifying how we're leaving our children to be raised in a world where they're worried about eating, worried about education, worried about their basic safety. And if you don't think that's going to affect young people, you're just fooling yourself. Of course it is. It's almost foreseeable that people put in a certain environment and forced to deal with daily traumas are going to react to that trauma. You know, we're sympathetic to trauma when it happens to a veteran who comes back from a horrifying experience in war. But somehow, we don't want to see it when it's happening to our youth growing up in our city. And so as a public defender, you're trying to sort of show that complexity of life in court. To say that there's more to these stories. That you are more than your worst act.

We do a poor job in the criminal legal system of addressing those underlying, structural issues, and then we punish the outcomes. And there are different reasons for this failure. Some jurisdictions, it's probably overt racism. Some jurisdictions, it's about economics and class. Some, it's about volume, just too many cases coming through. And there are obviously correlations and realities of poverty and race and gender. But if you talk to people involved in the system, they'll tell you the same stories: their mom is on drugs, and their dad is not there, and they're raising their siblings. They're like, *I had to make money. What am I going to do?* The alternative of selling drugs is better than losing their home or having their siblings taken from their family. What do you think is going to happen when faced with that choice? And if you follow the wrong path, if you take the only bad choice, why isn't that the society's fault for forcing that choice? A judge might say, *Well, you made that choice, son. You decided to go out there and sell drugs instead of going to school.* It is not just a personal choice, but a societal failure. This is about love, jobs, money, safety, and health. Right? It's what every person needs. And if you put those elements in the world where kids are at risk, you could change things for the better. It just takes money and will.

Yet, year after year, we don't make that investment. Instead, we sort of build out the criminal legal system to solve our social problems. We build drug courts, and not treatment facilities, and end up locking more people up. Think about it, if you went to a bunch of people with a lot of money and said, *Okay, your kids have a drug problem. Let's figure out a way to help your kids.* The top of that list is not going to be, you know, U.S. marshals, jail, and prison, right? It's going to be treatment, getting them out of the situation, finding a way—right? That's what you would do.

Instead, we sort of other-ize and create a reason for not caring. *Well, you forfeited your right. You did something bad.* When all the needs and lacks are still there. We bring people in to the criminal legal system as a measure of social control. We over-prosecute things that don't need to be prosecuted. We over-police places that don't need to be policed. And so we see a lot of people getting brought in pretty early into the system where others never would have. You know, having grown up in Washington, even if [my peers and I] had gotten caught for the stupid things we did, we would have been diverted. We never would have made it into the juvenile system. And that just doesn't happen if you're a young kid of color coming up in the same system, the same city.

I had this one client where it was a Title 16[1] case. He was 16 years old. And the facts alleged were that a kid went to his mom and said, "I just had my iPod stolen, and this kid (my client) pulled a gun on me and took my iPod." So police come. They arrest my client. No gun found. There's no real clear evidence of a gun at all. But because there's an allegation of a gun, this 16-year-old is charged as an adult in DC Superior Court. And a case that potentially could be a juvenile case where you end up with probation, or "I'm sorry I took your iPod..." becomes a Title 16 case with a 16-year-old kid facing 15 years for armed robbery as an adult. And he was lost throughout the whole trial. This world of confusion, where eventually you could just see him shrink and hide: you could see the impassive face.

And this case, which you would think would somehow get diverted—that some wise person would say, *Why is this case here? Why are we risking a 16-year-old's life on this iPod theft?*—goes to a full felony jury trial. The kid testifies. I thought we did a great job of showing that the allegation of the gun didn't come out until the other kid's mom was questioning her kid—like, "How did you lose your iPod? What do you mean he just took it from you?" And so the kid made up "Oh, he had a gun" to justify giving it away. The issue was never the theft, the facts showed he likely bullied the kid into giving up the iPod, but never had a gun. Anyway, so literally, the jurors, when they came back with a verdict, asked the judge, "Can the sentence be that he apologizes?" Saying, like, *That's what this should have been. Why didn't the moms work this out? That's what would happen in my world.* Right? Like, the mom should talk to the other mom and say: *I'm sorry. Can we have an apology? Can we move*

---

1   Title 16 refers to the DC code that states that juveniles can be charged as adults.

forward? Instead, we risked this kid's life for a felony armed robbery that was really a misdemeanor theft. It came out with the exact result that could have been resolved without the risk. And yet, this 16-year-old spent 100 days in DC Jail and was traumatized by it. I left thinking, *I did my job, justice was done, this is a good outcome.* And, like, maybe three months later, my client was arrested for murder.

From one perspective, the prosecutor probably was thinking, well, we should have locked him up for the armed robbery because now someone died. And then I'm thinking: How much of this is the damage of being inside the DC Jail as a 16-year-old and not knowing what to do? If you were 16 years old in DC Jail, and you want to survive, you have to be tough. All of the lessons of prison are the wrong lessons to succeed in society. I don't know exactly what happened; I didn't represent him for the second case. But maybe, had this first case not happened, we would have had a different outcome. These are the stories that reveal the complexity, the sadness, the tragedy, the impact on youth locked up as adults.

There are so many sentencings, especially in homicide cases, where you have a family who is about to lose a son to prison. And on the other side of the courtroom, a family who's lost a life to gun violence. It's a double loss, right? No matter what happens. And the two young men involved probably grew up within a mile of each other. They, for some reason, were sworn enemies for no apparent reason but neighborhood geography. The families recognize on one level that, but for the fortuity of who shot first, they would be in reversed roles. And yet, there's so much anger and so much sadness. As a defender, you're trying to argue for a minimization of sentencings or whatever the job entails, but the whole proceeding is missing the bigger picture: Why did these two 19-year-olds shoot at each other? Why have we allowed these cycles of violence to keep happening?

You know, most defender stories are tragedies. There are many times where you leave saddened by what you're seeing and the role you're playing. I had one client who was just 18 at the time he was sentenced for a 20-year sentence. He's in upstate New York right now in jail. And he's a wonderful kid. He's a young man with a smile that would light up a room. I'm not convinced he did the crime. The jury said he did. You know, I feel guilty. I keep thinking about him. On Christmas, I think of him. And I think of what it's like to lose 20 years of your life. And, I wonder, *Is it my fault?* I don't know. It's hard. I tried a good case. The judge was harsh. It's hard. It's sad.

Some lawyers are better at compartmentalizing. Some revert to red wine or whatever. Everyone has to find their own way of coping with that sadness. There's the legal way—obviously, you try to file the motions, and there's always an appeal, so there's always some hope for a criminal justice outcome. But the truth is that you have to figure out mechanisms in your own life to not let the sadness take over, not let it distract you from the next client or the next case. Which is, actually, part of the way of dealing with it. There is always another client, another case, another emergency, another crisis. And so, as a defender, there isn't that much time to wallow in the sadness of what the criminal legal system takes from the community, a theft which you could spend a lifetime thinking about.

This conversation piece has been edited since its original October 2021 publication.

My Hood

by Jekwan

I live in a place where there's no love,

    I come from a place where blood kills blood.

I live in a place where struggle is real,

    I come from a place where all you're taught is how to kill.

I live in a place where money is all that matters,

    I come from a place where disrespect will get your head shattered.

I live in a place where only the strong survive,

    I come from a place where a lot of my friends lost their lives.

I live in a place where many people don't understand,

    I come from a place where at 10 I had to be a man.

I live in a place where my family struggles to eat,

    I come from a place where the streets chose me.

I live in a place where I swore to die by the codes,

    I come from a place where violence is getting old.

I live in a place where I don't want my kids to go,

    I come from a place where I swear by Allah,

I don't want my baby boys to grow...

The City of 202
by Jarod

The city of 202[1]
Got so much love
But who really riding 4 you?
Despite the Capitol, the monument and the White House
There is so much that your eyes wouldn't have a clue
The city of 202
Might be so beautiful
But mostly everything you see isn't true
And everything that happens isn't posted in the news
The city of 202
Got so much love
But who really riding 4 you?

---

1   202 is the area code for Washington, DC.

My Projects
by Andre

I come from a place where we
Live like a savage to see another day
And nobody takes the time to show
Us a better way
Life ain't easy in my projects
Heroin, needles, and desert eagles
Is all we see
And mentally worse than what you see
On TV
My chest feels hollow
Hope I make it to tomorrow
Trying to cope with the pain
Of the fast lane
My grandma praying that I walk
Through the door
'Cause she heard about a youngster
Laid out by the store
Now you see that life ain't
Easy in my projects
You rather get it from me
Than go by TV

Things of That Nature

by Derrick C.

Yeah they say I grew up where I'm not wanted.
Where my surroundings were beautiful,
and all the others growing looked different than me.

But who's to blame?
Cause I know I was planted here for a reason.
Even if the world don't know or see.

They trust all the others,
with their pretty faces that just make you give them attention.

And their sharp bodies that make people be careful how they handle them,
if touching them is their intention.

Who's to say I'm not just as beautiful, and deserve some respect and power?
Cause even though they're roses and I'm a dandelion,
I'm still considered a flower.

(IMPRISONMENT)

This chapter includes poetry and prose that illuminate
the dehumanization and desperation imposed by forced,
physical confinement. Included is the perspective of a
correctional officer alongside the poetry of incarcerated
and formerly incarcerated youth, to show the different
ways the system impacts all those connected to it—the
physical response and the mental adjustments, the
intentional shifts in mindset and viewpoint required to
survive and, sometimes, transcend the walls.

I Will Cry for the Little Boy

by Halim

After "Who Will Cry for the Little Boy?" by Antwone Fisher

I will cry for the little boy
In shackles and away from home
I will cry for the little boy
Trapped in a cell all alone

I will cry for the little boy
Whose heart is too cold to weep
I will cry for the little boy
Pain never lets him sleep

I will cry for the little boy
He was buried alive in the burning sand
I will cry for the little boy
The boy sentenced to life like a man

I will cry for the little boy
Who knows his soul is in chains
I will cry for the little boy
His spirit died again and again

I will cry for the little boy
A good boy he tried to be
I will cry for the little boy
That died inside of me

Me siento solo

por Carlos

Me encuentro a mi mismo creciendo
en un sistema judicial
y no en la casa con mis padres, si no creciendo
cada día en la cárcel
esto me hace sentirme de menos.

Las personas empiezan a olvidarse
de mi y de mis problemas se olvidan
que soy un humano más que cometió
un error.

Las personas se olvidan de mi
cada día más, me tratan como un criminal
tengo miedo pasar mi vida en la cárcel.
Me siento solo en la cárcel.

Y no puedo cambiar lo que hice
siento que el sistema judicial
no quiere dejarme ir,
siento como que quieren dejarme aquí,
como que si no tuviera vida o familia.
Me siento solo en la cárcel.

I Feel Alone

by Carlos

I find myself growing up
in a judicial system
and not at home with my parents,
growing every day in prison
makes me feel less than human.

People start to forget
they forget about me and my problems
that I am human
and more than a mistake I committed.

People forget about me more
Every day, they treat me like a criminal
I am afraid to spend my life in prison.
I feel alone in prison.

And I can't change what I did
I feel that the judicial system
does not want to let me go,
I feel like it wants to leave me here,
as if I did not have a life or a family.
I feel alone in prison.

A Cell

by Johnny

A metal bunk bed
A mattress and hard pillow
Two lockers and one desk
A toilet and sink

A door that is closed
Heat out the vent and it's hot
I'm sweating, yet it's cold
A night light on, yet it's dark

A sheet covers me
Yet I want more than a sheet
The floor is cold
Yet I need more than heat

A window, but it's closed
A mirror, but it's fogged
A mind full of thoughts
A heart of love that feels clogged

A rush to go, yet I'm here
I say I smile, but it's a tear
I say I'm relaxed, but I'm tense
I say I'm free, but see a fence

Jonas
(essay)

There I sat in the "hole," also known as the Secure Housing Unit. The cell was small and dim. The bed was maybe a foot off the floor, and it felt like I might as well be sleeping on the ground. There was a window in this particular cell, though it was caged off, and I really couldn't see anything except for the barbed wire fence of the juvenile prison where I was being housed. The occasional patrol van slowly cruised around the compound while I would stand there, sometimes for hours, just gazing out the window at nothing. Longing for the day I'd taste freedom again, imagining everything I'd do given half the chance. Gazing out of that caged off window helped me escape (at least for a little while) the torture of being confined to that cell 23 hours a day. The tier was loud as usual, filled with the voices of boys joning, telling war stories, making plans for the future and threatening each other's lives! The boy right next to me was calling to another boy two cells down and across from us.

"Choppa! A Lil Choppa!"

"What!" Choppa answered.

"Bring your lil anteater-lookin'-*ss to the door." Some of the boys on the tier laughed.

"Whatchu want?"

"I'm tryna holla at you cuz," my next-door neighbor said, sounding very sincere.

"Ain't nobody f*ckin' witchu right now. Press that bunk, with your Beetlejuice lookin'-*ss. I'm tryna read over here." More laughter from the boys on the tier.

"You might as well come kick it, cuz you know d*mn well you can't read!" My neighbor said, bursting out laughing along

with the other boys listening.

Their voices faded out as I tuned into another conversation somewhere on the tier.

"When I get outta here bruh I ain't never comin back, straight up. This ain't about to be my life," one boy said.

"Yeah, I'm witchu on that. My uncle just came home after 10 years and he studying right now to get his CDL[1] license so he can drive trucks. I'ma do the same thing, that way I'll make enough money to take care of my daughter and be able to travel."

"Yeah, I think I want to go back to school too," the first boy responded. I began thinking maybe I'd like to go back to school myself, but there was one big difference between me and most of the other boys. The longest sentence between them didn't exceed 10 years, and their sentences were parolable, so the average stay for any of them was 12 to 24 months. Me, on the other hand, well I was in a totally different boat. I was a federal juvenile who'd been sentenced to a 40-year, nonparolable sentence, being housed in their state juvenile prison until I was old enough to be transferred to federal prison. That's what my future looked like, and with that thought, I dismissed the idea of going back to school. Hey, I could always read about and hear about other people's college experience.

On this day in particular, one of the boys started kicking and banging on his door, which wasn't unusual at all. Here and there guys would get restless, or just break down from being locked in a cage like a wild animal, and kicking and banging on the door, and sometimes screaming at the top of your lungs was the only means of releasing some of the trauma we were experiencing. I walked to the cell door to look out of the window and saw that it was the boy across the hall

1   Commercial Driver's License

from me. I knew him. We were both in the Juvenile Cognitive Intervention Program Unit. It was known for housing most of the kids with mental health issues. He was a 14-year-old Native American kid who was normally full of jokes, eager to make you smile. He was also on some type of medication. He kicked and banged on the door for about two hours before one of the C.O.'s or "Youth Counselors" (YCs) as they were called, came down the hallway.

"What's your problem?"

"I need to talk to somebody!" the boy screamed.

"It's after four o'clock, the psych department's gone, and the chaplain too."

"What? Man, I need to talk to somebody!"

"Well, too bad."

The YC completely dismissed the situation and walked off. The boy yelled every obscenity at him, cursing and calling him everything but a Child of God. He continued to kick and bang. Another hour went by and now the YCs were starting to serve the dinner trays. When the YC got to his door with his tray he opened the tray slot and asked, "Are you gonna keep banging and being disruptive?"

"Man, f*ck you!" the boy responded.

We had hot dogs and tater tots that night. The YC took the boy's hot dogs off his tray and licked all over them, placed them back on his tray slot, and then locked it.

"Enjoy," the YC said, as the boy exploded with newfound energy. He kicked and banged and screamed like the devil was in the cell with him.

I noticed that the other YC working the block didn't see him lick the hot dogs because he was on the other side of the unit passing food out, and spitting on the food would leave clear evidence of foul play, so licking the hot dogs was his way of being vindictive and safeguarding himself at the same

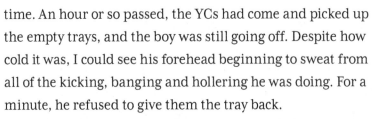

time. An hour or so passed, the YCs had come and picked up the empty trays, and the boy was still going off. Despite how cold it was, I could see his forehead beginning to sweat from all of the kicking, banging and hollering he was doing. For a minute, he refused to give them the tray back.

"I ain't givin y'all sh*t!" he screamed, spittle flying from his mouth onto the window of his door. "This my d*mn tray, now get the f*ck away from my door!" he taunted, and then moments later he threw the tray on the floor for them to pick up. A half hour later the two YCs working the unit came down the hallways to the boy's cell, along with three or four other patrolmen. We could hear their keys rattling way before they got down the hallways. A few boys yelled, "Goon squad comin'!"

"Here come the goon squad!"

I became a little anxious thinking about what was going to happen next. The staff liked to do things like taking everyone's rec time the following day on account of one person. It was a tactic they used to manipulate the majority to turn on the one guy or a few guys. But at that moment I was more concerned with whether or not they were going to start spraying mace on the tier. That always sucked because then I'd have to take my shirt off, soak it in water, wring it out some, then wrap it around my face in order to minimize how much of the mace I inhaled. But that's all it did was minimize it, because I'd still suffer a coughing fit that would last hours until all the mace had aired out. I braced myself. They went into the boy's cell. He wasn't very big, about 5 foot 5, 140 pounds, but he had the heart of a lion because with no hesitation he began throwing punches. Both YCs and all the patrolmen were at least 6 feet tall and 200 pounds. He fought to no avail. The YCs and patrolmen walked right through his punches, one grabbed him up in a chokehold while another took hold of his legs. "Get off me! Get the f*ck off me!" He screamed as he struggled against them. The others removed his bedding and mattress.

They put him down then pushed him to the ground and left the cell. He was so angry now he was crying. He still kicked and banged continuously.

Another hour passed, and the goon squad returned. This time they restrained him, stripped him completely naked and removed the clothes from the cell. He stood at the door and continued to cry and scream for another five minutes, then he suddenly stopped. He disappeared from the window. It was winter time, and I knew he had to be as cold as ice with nothing on and nothing to cover up with. Everyone else I could see from my window, including myself, were wrapped up in their blankets because it was so cold in the cell. The boy remained silent. I imagined he was shivering, teeth chattering. More silence.

"I'm sorry!" the boy screamed frantically. He was sniffling and his voice cracked.

"I ain't gonna do it not more! I'm sorry!" He kept yelling this out until the YCs eventually returned his clothes and bedding. Afterward, a strange silence covered the tier. The whole time this situation was taking place, I was trying to ignore it, but I couldn't. I was all too familiar with the rage, confusion, and panic I knew the boy was experiencing. I tried to fight it, but it was rising up within and my defenses were not yet strong enough. I broke down. My lips began to quiver uncontrollably, my eyes welled up with tears, and I clenched my fist in a vain attempt to restrain the flood that was surely coming. Once the tears began to pour, they seemed as if they would never stop. I was suddenly exhausted. I sat down. Thoughts of the past haunted me. I was forced to confront and acknowledge all the terrible things I had done, all the horrible things I'd experienced. Not even sleep could offer me an escape because I would have dreams where I was fighting or running for my life. In either scenario, I would always jump up out of my sleep breathing hard, sometimes sweating. I was

forced to navigate the wilderness of my own mind.

Through my tears and quiet sobs, I began to find myself.

This was my third time in the hole, and I was beginning to accept my past for what it was, and recognize the disguised blessings it had left me with. I began to accept the fact that these so-called "YCs" were doing everything in their power to alienate us from our humanity. However, through a gift of understanding, I realized that they were only debasing themselves. I began to understand that the only way out of the fire was through it, and a certain contentment came with this realization. I began to find peace, despite the circumstances, for perhaps the first time in my life. It dawned on me that the boy and I were both soldiers for the same struggle; the only difference was he exploded while I imploded. I decided right then and there that this wasn't going to define my life, and that I wouldn't be defeated. I would put forth a conscious effort to be more proactive. More importantly, I decided that I wanted to change. I wanted to be better. I made up my mind that the time I spent in prison would not be in vain, and I knew I was strong enough to handle whatever came my way. Thoughts of my future all of a sudden became that much brighter, and with this came newfound resolve. I wiped the tears from my eyes, took a deep breath, opened *The Autobiography of Malcolm X*, and started reading.

Jonas was released under DC's Incarceration Reduction Amendment Act in September 2020 after 17 years behind bars beginning at age 16. He is a production assistant for a social impact production company and media consulting firm. He recently published his own collection of poetry, *Mastering the Pain*.

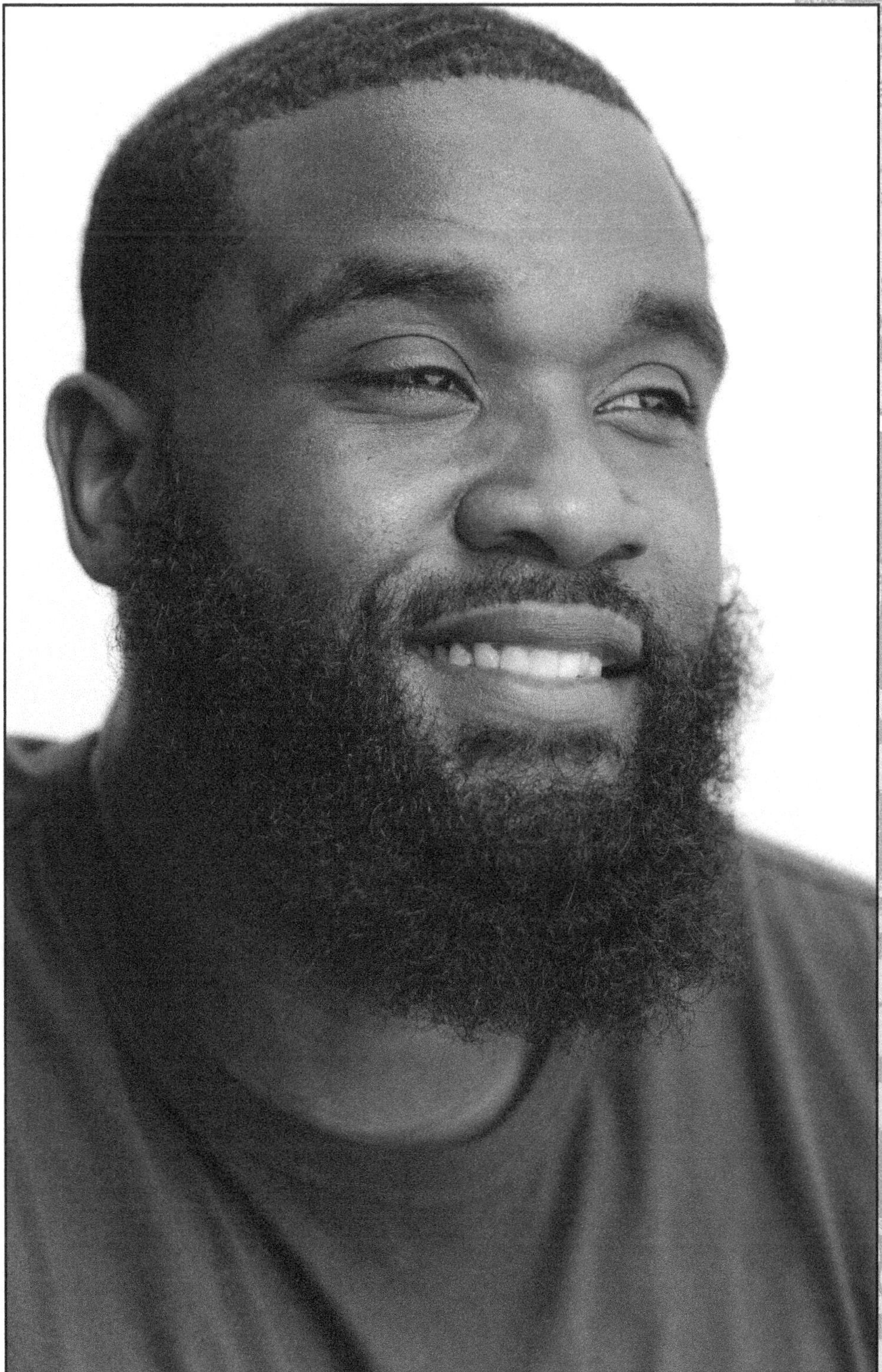

Looking Out My Cell Window

by Shawn

Each morning is the most amazing experience I have

Each morning when I awake and before I lay down for the night

There's abundance of pigeons that hang out by the steps, I love to see them
    take flight

I've named a few of them and I'd like to think they know it

I feed them when I go to insulin line with pockets full of breadcrumbs, wow
    they just love it

At night when the compound's settled and everything's on lockdown

There's this little black and white skunk that loves to come around

I imagine sometimes that this little guy is me

And I just walk to the gate, go right under not even needing a key

Sometimes it rains here, and the rain runs down the glass

I pray because I've always thought rain was God's tears on those day that
    he's sad

Looking out my cell window is another world, even though I can go out
    when they call a move

But when I look from my cell, it's like it only belongs to me and my heart
    is soothed

What do you see when you look out your front room window today?

Untitled

by Daniel P.

I am trapped in a cell with no possibility of being free

Free Minds is me

For as I close my eyes, nature appears in front of me

The sweet smell of flowers and the lovely birds that sing

Allah has blessed not only me, but also the animals that are free

Nature is to me a place for all to see

It's the beauty of the sky and the ground beneath my feet that holds

A mystery present for all to see

Nature isn't me, but I am trapped

In a cell with no possibility of being free

When I close my eyes this is nature to me

Freedom

by Donte

It ain't nothing better than freedom

Until you lose it

In the streets with a virus

It must be for a young African American like me

Easy to catch a case

Like a short grace

You in the streets

You blink twice

You on your way to a cage in the pen

Pics of your kid every now and then

Walking around with a wrist band

Six digits and a food tray in your hand

Wondering, will you get your freedom again

Sharon
(conversation)

It's not easy work. There have been people that come to
corrections with a smile. They don't smile anymore. You
know? The job has made them so hard. Hard in their hearts
and their mind. Conforming to what other officers do
that's not right. And then you have those that it's all about
corrections. I always tell my staff, corrections means to
correct when necessary. Not just because you can. So, if you
take that badge, and you misuse it, you know, these inmates,
they realize who really is about them and who is not. These
kids know that.

I used to work on the juvenile unit at the DC Jail, before they
changed the law. Now the kids are in juvenile detention
even though they're charged as adults, but back then they
were on a unit at the jail. A lot of times, we find officers on
that unit that don't really have the passion to work with
kids. It's disheartening. Because you look at them, their
communication skills, they don't really know how to talk to
these kids. I mean, if a kid says "f*** you" to you, and you say
"f*** you" back, who is the professional? Who is the adult?
You know what I'm saying? Now, on the other hand, Miss
Hargrove would have said, "Am I speaking to you like that,
son? We're not going to get anything accomplished with you
cussing at me." That's the way I'm going to start off. Because
you've got to start at that level. Okay, if it escalates, then
maybe my voice, my tone, might get a little stern. That hasn't
happened a lot because they had a lot of respect for me. And
I had respect for them.

Sharon shares her perspective as a correctional officer.

I wrote a proposal to implement a program called the AOAT – Adjusting Our Attitude Training program. The warden said, "Well, Hargrove, I really like this proposal. But I'm going to ask that you go to the worst block in this facility to implement it." People said that it wouldn't work, everyone was telling me how bad these kids were. But I spoke to them and let them know that there was going to be a program on this block. One of the kids said, "We ain't doing no motherf***ing program." One of the others, he said, "You know they killed a police out there in the community. You're not scared?" I said, "The Lord is my light and my salvation whom should I fear?" And I looked around at all of them. I said, "It's not you, not you, not you, not you." I said, "Monday morning, be in formation." And it got quiet. It got really quiet.

Monday morning, I came in. None of them were in formation. [Laughs.] And the second day, none of them were in formation. Now, the warden had given me rein, but I had to get them to make this program work, right? I said, "Do you want to be somebody? Or do you want to be in those cells? If you want a program, come on out here. Because I'm going to give you some knowledge." Eventually there was about four of them that came out in formation. So I started working with those four. The next thing you know, four turned into eight, and then eight turned into 48 before the week was over. They were in formation, all of them. And it was on and popping.

The following week, they were starting to take ownership of their cells. I'm talking about keeping their cells clean. Coming to formations on time. We were facilitating groups. We spoke about anything and everything as far as manhood. We talked about STDs. Suicide. Victims' impact. Conflict resolution. But what they liked the most was count time. That used to be one

of the problems on the unit. And let me tell you why they liked count time so much: I played music.

But it wasn't always hip-hop; it wasn't what they wanted to hear. One day, I played some jazz while they were in doing the count. And it was, like, "Miss Hargrove, who is that?" I said, "Oh, boy, you don't know nothing about that." Right? The second day, I played gospel. It was a nice, catchy beat to it. And it's, like, "Who is that?" I said, "Oh, man, you guys don't know nothing about that." The third day, I believe it was some Barbra Streisand, Chicago, Kiss, and all that. And they were, like, "Man, come on, what you doing, Miss Hargrove?" They had no choice but to hear it, but they were quiet, they were listening, and they were curious. So on Friday after playing all this music, we spoke about cultural diversity. It was a good group.

A lot of times, the approach just has to be different. Like, for an example, how did I get them to do PT?[1] By giving them basic education and PT at the same time. I told them they had to learn the capitals of every state. What's the capital of Florida? Tallahassee. Okay. Pennsylvania? Harrisburg. Vermont? Montpelier. They had to know these states. I asked them to learn maybe 10 capitals each night. If they didn't know it, then they had to give me 20 push-ups. So if I asked one of them, "What's the capital of New York?" and they didn't say "Albany," they had to give me 20 Albanies: One-Albany, two-Albany, three-Albany... They didn't want to be wrong. But at the same time, it didn't make them feel like someone was making them do it. It was a game to them. Right? So not only are they getting basic education, they're also doing PT at the same time. And they loved it. It's the approach.

1   Physical Training

You've got to first touch people's mindset. It's not easy at first, but first and foremost, they have to know that you really care. It's not just a job. They knew that I was there about them. It's not about being authoritative. It's: *This is what I really want for you guys. I want you to be successful.* You know? I picked that up the first time I called one of them "son." But I ended up calling all of them "son." I knew all of their names. But I still called them "son"—each and every one of them. Especially if they were doing something wrong. You say, "Son, you know you can't do that." They liked that.

I felt like I couldn't do more because—how do I say this? I work for an agency. And there are still rules and regulations and guidelines within our agency. If it was up to me, I would have did more. I really didn't want to leave. But I had enough of them not supporting my program. I could have did a whole lot more with support. I wanted some musical instruments. We had kids I wanted to put some drumsticks in their hands. And some drums. And let them play. If it was up to me, they might have been able to have a band up in there. They're so gifted, some of them. But they didn't even know how much a gift they had because no one really exposed them to their gift. Because when you start sitting around, you're talking in group, they start learning a lot about themselves and then other people—young men on the unit. Which kept them from fighting one another. It kept them from assaulting officers. Because they were being productive. They were doing something.

The first time I went back over there after I left the juvenile unit, they were, like, "Miss Hargrove?" I said "Oorah." Because I'd say "Oorah" to them a lot. (I was military.) They didn't say it back. I said, *What's up with that?* So before I left out the door, I said, "Y'all didn't give me no love today, huh?" And they

said, "Yeah, because you left us." You know, because they've been abandoned. And then I sat them down in a group and I explained to them, "Don't you all want to see me do better? Just like I want to see you do better. Don't you want the good things for me in life?" And they were like, "Yeah, yeah, you're right. Respect. Respect." I said, "I'll come over and hit y'all up every now and then." And they was, like, "Okay, all right. It's cool." And then I said, "Oorah," and they said "OORAH!"

It's all about respect.

Human

by CXS

I wear my hair low because you say so

My eyes see your light even when darkness abounds

My smile is not sincere but it's what's required

My ears have never heard "you love me" even though
they continue to listen for the sound

My shoulders are broad so you know that I'm strong,
but my arms are weak because pain is heavy

My chest ink covers the stories the streets tell,
gun shots, and stab wounds are not fiction

My legs are tired of walking from one home to another,
but my feet would walk off the earth for that permanent place
of refuge

My back carries what was loaded onto it but not asked for

This is what makes me human, I'm waiting for you to acknowledge
the same.

When

by Lydell

I wake
to the sun rising in the East
the rays burning my eyes
as I shake off the sleep

My first vision is bars
before a screen and a half open window
beyond that is cages
a gun tower and twenty-foot wall

Then I see something else, everyday
that should give hope to all
high upon a pole, it waves at me
sometimes to the East, sometimes to the West

Surrounded by blue skies and white clouds
both symbols of freedom
both symbols of life
today I feel neither, tomorrow will be the same

I am of the world, but not in it
so I stare out the window and wonder, WHEN
when will I live my life in this manner
of life, of liberty, and the pursuit of happiness

WHEN, I ponder as I look at the Star-Spangled Banner

The Beast

by Gordon

Free me from the beast that holds the minds of many. Free me from that terrifying Roar which lies within me. Though it's in a cage, it still shows his teeth. Silently waiting to attack those who caused grief. It sweats constantly and beads form around its brow. Yet it never alters only nourishes the thoughts of relieving its hunger like that of a crying child.

Free me from the Beast that turns men into Savages. Free me from a place where every day is tragic. Laws are in place to punish and tame. But evil begets evil, so immorality remains. The walls close in, and the heart begins to pound. How can one amend, when the soul is broken down.

Free me from the beast that tells these awful tales. Free me from the coffin that's designed as a cell. Is there such thing as Beauty in the world when all that surrounds the vision is hell? How can one survive with no sense of touch, taste, sight, or smell. If survival is key, life has led me astray. I no longer sleep; I die at the end of each day.

Free me from the Beast that forbids me to mourn. Free me from the screams of those who have long gone. Contemplating with each year that passes by. Suicide is not the first reaction. The inside has already died. No more dreams; no more goals; yes, there's blood in my eyes. Men don't hold secrets; we secretly past lies.

Free me from the Beast that drains the mind of ambition. Free me from the binary chains of that we call religion. We must have killed God because the prince is winning. When you look at me, can you see my Venom? There are no fangs or peeled off skin but at times I slither. No natural selection, this evolution is richer. Free me from the Beast that I have grown to love. Free me from the home that I no longer think of.

Trapped

by Curtis M.

Prison stands in stark contrast

Out front manicured fresh green grass

They do that to impress the upper class

But what about the other half

Black community viewed as the lower class

Thrown in prison like alley trash

They had it all backwards

Instead of treating the disease

They spend millions on treating the symptoms

Years later I now understand the politics of it all

We were set up to fail

Leave us in the hood to smash right into DC Jail's brick walls

THE LAND OF BROKEN SOULS

(SOLITARY CONFINEMENT)

The writing in this chapter describes the experience of solitary
confinement that drives the authors to despair, regret, and,
sometimes, the edge of suicide. A conjured memory or a secret
smile can distract, but it is a fleeting respite. Incarcerated and
formerly incarcerated poets and essayists speak to how this
deprivation affects the body, spirit, and mind.

Lost But Not Found

by Juan

Lost but not found

Tryna swim but still I drown

My smiles turn to frowns

My teardrops shake the ground

My heart weighs a ton

These walls are closing in but I can't run

My ears are bleeding from the sounds of screams

My neighbors yelling Momma help me

This hole is caving in and my mind is vanishing

Suicidal thoughts going through my mind is just rambling

And my self-pride and sanity is leaking from my soul

And two feet to my left is a commode

Two feet to my right is where my head goes

No food no books and no telephone

Men cry and shout we all just wanna go home

Cry for help falls on deaf ears, no one's home

Should I tie up my bed sheets, jump, and just let life go

Might as well, feels like no one loves me anymore

This is a place where no one would dare go

This is called the SHU[1] aka the land of the broken souls

---

1   Secure Housing Unit, also known as solitary confinement

Staring at the Wall
by Curtis W.

I was warned there'd be times like these

But nothing could've prepared me for Dr. S.

Who comes around once a week

Peeking in my cell like he knows me better than I know myself

I'll bet he gets a kick out of seeing a 22-year-old

Who has been locked away in a cell since he was 16

Who has 30 more to go if a blessing doesn't come through this d*mn wall

That he's been staring at for the past 6 hours

I often come to this wall to somewhat free my mind

Or to drown out my annoying cellie

Who can't stop talking about his boring relationship with his girlfriend

He can't seem to stop fighting

Even though she calls the cops on him every time

Or sometimes when the lights go out and the prison raucous is done for the day

I guess to seek mental refuge from this place

Other times just to reflect on what life was like before 23 and 1

When it was cookouts, huggies and hamburgers

Yeah, that always brings a smile to my face

Lately that's been the routine

I start reflecting and end up with this smile

Staring at this d*mn wall!

Then here comes this Dr. wanting to know why I'm sitting here smiling at
the wall

I give him the usual, "Nothing"

But to be honest

I smile to keep from crying

Solitary Confinement

by Earl

Speaking uncut
Ima tell it raw
Gon tell you how it is
In the SHU[1] behind the wall
Wearing people's clothes
Other people's draws
Working for some cents
In the streets won't get a job
Hour worth of rec
In a cage like a dog
CO's[2] mad at one
And they take it out on all
Yeah, Feds play dirty
No commissary
One call a month
Why my family worry
Lunch at ten o'clock
Tell me ain't that too early
Trays half filled
'Cause they made 'em in a hurry
Some dude's fury
Some stay silent
That's the way it is
Locked in solitary confinement

1 Secure Housing Unit, also known as solitary confinement
2 Correctional Officer

Antwon, age 19

Antwon
(conversation)

I knew the judge was going to give me a lot of time. In the beginning, all of us felt like we could do it, you know, because we was living that type of life. I got 93 years. Even when I heard my sentence, I didn't think nothing of it. When I went back to the bullpen though, it hit me. At that moment, I realized I would probably die in prison. I was 19.

That was 11 years ago. I wouldn't say that I have adapted to the reality, or really learned to deal with the time. I just don't think about it, you know. Because when I think about it, there are moments of temporary insanity.

I've spent at least seven of the last 11 years in solitary confinement. One time, I did a year and a half straight. Being in solitary, it can do something to your brain. It's just traumatizing. I've seen people break down. I've heard them yell all night. Scream and bang on the door until they physically can't do it no more. You know that part in the Bible, that says something like: "With much wisdom comes much sorrow; the more knowledge, the more grief?" That's how I feel when I hear people banging in solitary. Now that I have the knowledge and understanding, it hurts me to know human beings are subjected to that kind of abuse.

It breaks people. One way or the other. What I mean by that, I know it sounds weird, but sometimes I actually welcome the chance to be alone. I'm beginning to think I might like it *too* much. You can get addicted to solitary. Then when you

come back out to general population and have to be around other people, that's when the problems come up. That's how it is for me. It's really hard to adjust to being back in general population. To be without human contact for that length of time can make you emotionally imbalanced. When I come out, I don't like people walking close to me, bumping me, or talking with their hands. Every time, I have to relearn how to be with other people.

Reading and writing give me a sanctuary when I'm in solitary. I didn't learn to read and write until I was 16 years old at the DC Jail. I've read more than 100 books in prison. *The Autobiography of Malcolm X* taught me that every man can redeem himself, that just because you come to prison doesn't mean it's over for you. You can still do great things. Some people say, *If you want to hide something from a Black man, put it in a book.* Well now that I can read, I read to understand. I can't stop and I won't stop. Writing is my backbone. If it weren't for me writing poetry, I don't think I could have made it through. It's full of pain at times, but my life is painful. Writing helps me to cope and to forgive.

When you're in solitary, you spend a lot of time looking in the mirror. And that's when you start to notice things. The gray hairs, the wrinkles in your face. You're forced to think about what you don't have. What you love. What you lost. You think about your family and you wonder, *How did I get here?*

I was 12 years old when I got locked up the first time. I tried to rob a guy for his jacket and they sent me to Oak Hill.[1] Kids younger than 13 weren't allowed to touch the yard or mix with

---

1   Oak Hill was the District's juvenile facility that was closed in 2009 after a lawsuit proved that the conditions were inhumane and abusive.

older kids. So they put me on solitary. At the time, I welcomed it. I thought this is what's supposed to happen. Half the guys I was hanging with had already been there, so I thought by me going to the juvenile facility and getting locked down, it solidified my place in the community, you know? I wore it like a badge of honor.

I look back on the brother that I used to be, and I don't like him. He was so ignorant and so foolish. I don't like who I used to be when I got to prison, and that's why I changed. I pray, I read, I write, and I have educated myself. The way I care about other people now, the way I react, the way I think and the way I carry myself—I'm different.

I understand that I am a product of what I came from. The crime that I committed was my fault, and mine alone. But now I understand so much more why I did what I did. Because I was taught how to hate more than love. I was taught how to survive in the wrong ways.

If I could talk to that 12-year-old boy sitting in that cell at Oak Hill, I'd tell him your mother loves you. I would tell him it was her addiction to heroin that had her moving like that. I would tell him that your father wasn't taught how to be a man. It was his inexperience that made him like that. I would tell him you are loved regardless of your situation. I would tell him to put God first. I would tell him to stay in school. I would tell him that he is worth it.

But I don't have the right to sorrow. I don't have a right to ask God, *Why me?* A lot of people say they want to help the youth to teach them. I want to work with youth because I feel like I owe them. I owe a lot of people.

My dream is to get out of prison. My goal is to become a writer. What I really want to do is ask my victim's mother for forgiveness. Just tell her that I'm sorry.

Antwon is incarcerated in a high-security US Penitentiary. His poems have been published in *The Paragon Journal* and *Tacenda Literary Magazine*. His scheduled release date is in 2093.

Artificial Elements

by Marquis

Naturally brown-skinned, but

Turned pale from lack of sunlight

Haven't seen the moon in many moons

Entombed by elements holding me hostage

Some cement, sand, gravel, whipped with water

Makes these walls of concrete

Iron treated with intense fire made this steel

Restricting my hands and feet

Only breeze I can feel comes from a dusty vent

Perverted minds twisted nature's true intent

Instead of nature's nurture

Deprivation of nature

Is a form of torture

Slight relief comes through a rec cage

Where I glimpse the heavens for one hour

Yearning to feel the rain

I settle in this all-aluminum shower

A shame that seasons continue to change

I only view these bare cells

That stay the same

WHEN THE SKY BLINKS

(LOVE)

The poetry and prose of incarcerated and formerly incarcerated people and their loved ones reveals the power of love and longing for another, separated by years and bars. The concept of love, in isolation, can bring beauty and joy. The focus on these emotions serves as resistance in an environment designed for punishment.

When the Sky Blinks

by Rafael

Will you meet me when the sky blinks, under its blinded gaze, where
    thousands of lights gleam?
Amongst nature's silky voice, surrounded by clicks, croaks, howls,
    and whistles...
Will you meet me?
To bask in its beauty, to sit enjoying this moment of glory which this
    blink brings...
When the sky blinks
Mysteries are seen, excitement stirs in the air and everything is waiting
    for you to discover it...
Will you meet me when the sky blinks?
To dance to nature's song, to twirl and laugh under its luminous glow...
Tell me will you meet me?
With the wind whispering in our ears, the sweet caress of the breeze,
    imaginations running wild...
Only when the sky blinks
Will you meet me when the sky blinks?
Where myths are made and games are played, you hide, I seek and when
    we meet...
So much fun happens when the sky blinks
Will you accept my invitation? Will we meet at the time the sky blinks?
I assure you everything will be amazing...
Will you meet me when the sky blinks?
I will give you time for contemplation, yet hurry we have depleted
    our duration
Just give me a wink to let me know that we will meet...
When the sky blinks

Luis
(conversation)

I was born in Mexico, but we moved to El Salvador when I was about three. My father had diabetes. When I was eight, he passed away. My mom had to provide for me and my brother. We were poor. Where we lived, it wasn't even a house. In Spanish, they call them *champas*. It's slang for "hut" or "shack." They're just pieces of propped up sheet metal. There was no bathroom or running water. We didn't know anything different though. We had fun flying kites. We played soccer barefoot with a ball made out of plastic. And school was all about fun times. We were happy kids.

After my father died, my mom wanted to come to the United States because we were getting older and it was getting dangerous in El Salvador. The gangs were growing and it was very violent. She tried to save up for the trip, but it was impossible. She worked at a flea market, selling t-shirts. But she couldn't even afford to pay for her own stall. She had to walk up and down the streets to sell her merchandise under the hot sun. She was making $7.50 a day—maybe $12 on a really good day. Finally, she borrowed money from friends so we could make the trip. I remember seeing her holding a Ziploc bag full of money.

First, we went to Guatemala by bus, and then to Mexico City. From there we travelled north to Sonora. It was just the three of us. I was 10 and my brother was 11. My mom got in contact with people who would help us cross the desert. They assured us that we wouldn't walk that much and we would only walk

at night. But it's a desert, so at night it's actually really cold, and that's when the animals come out to hunt. We saw coyotes, snakes, rats, all kinds of animals.

At that age, my brother and I didn't really see the danger in what we were doing. We saw it more like a field trip—an adventure. If you try to make the same trip now, there's a 99% chance you will be kidnapped and sold from one criminal organization to another. But back then, the smugglers were more honest, and they cared about the kids, which was lucky for us, I guess. I know my mother was scared though.

During the day we would rest. We ate canned tuna, tortillas, chickpeas, sardines, you know, anything that was easy to carry. When the sun set, that's when we started walking. It took three days. We were still deep in the desert when some people in our group got hurt—I think one of them broke their ankle. The leader warned us before we started, that we couldn't risk the entire group if one person couldn't keep up. So we left them. I guess they had to turn around and go back.

Once we made it to the American side, they loaded up a small truck with like 20-30 people. It was about an 11-hour drive to a safe house in Phoenix. Then they divided us up depending on where we were headed. From there, my mom, my brother, and I drove to Virginia with two men in a pick-up truck.

I think my brother and I loved everything about America when we first saw it. It was all so new and exciting to us.

We moved to a crowded apartment in Southeast DC. There were only three Latinos in my middle school. An 8th grade kid, my brother in 7th, and me in 6th. Everyone else was

Black. I didn't understand what was happening in class because it was in English. On top of that, I was behind because I'd missed two years of school. I started skipping class. I got into a public charter high school and that was much more diverse. The people were friendly. But outside of school it was a totally different story. I learned that violence was the only way to be respected in the streets. I got picked on because I didn't speak English and because I was seen as different. I kept having to defend myself.

The gangs don't even have to recruit young Latino kids. It all started with a game of soccer. You can just be playing a regular soccer game with a bunch of kids. But now you've been seen with kids who are in a gang, and now you have enemies. And nobody's going to believe you when you say that you're not part of it. You're already caught up and it's too late.

I was 16 when I was arrested and charged with a felony. Prison put a stop on me. It's hard to say that being incarcerated actually helped me, because prison doesn't provide anything helpful. I was placed in a high security facility where we were almost always on lockdown, so there weren't many programs available to me. I read every book that I could get my hands on. I also wrote a lot of poetry. I didn't want all of my poems to be sad or about life in prison. So I wrote love poems. Even though there was no love in my life, creating love poems gave me the inspiration to write, to dream, to live. It gave me something to hang on to.

Being incarcerated is what you make of it. It can be a university for life, or it can be a training ground to become a lifelong criminal. I chose to use it as a wake-up call. I woke up and realized what I wanted from my life. And it wasn't this.

I served 10 years in prison. Instead of being released, I was transferred to an ICE[1] facility to wait to be deported. It was scary. I felt so alone. My brother and mother, who had remained in DC for a few years, had since left the US. I didn't know how or when we might ever be reunited. Imagine you've been locked up for 10 years and you're being sent to a country where you don't know anyone or anything. When I arrived in Mexico that first day, I was truly in a foreign country. I felt like I didn't belong. I had nothing to eat. I had no place to go. And where I was in Mexico, every place is potentially dangerous. Everything you see on the news, it's true.

More than anything, I was afraid of the police. Because when the cops come up to you, it's never about anything good! And here, there is no such thing as justice. It's all about the money. If they can get money out of you, they will. The other day, I saw them beating up a civilian. There was one guy holding him and three more kicking him, and the dude was face down and already handcuffed. I went into a store and on the way back 10 minutes later, they were still on top of him beating him. I felt bad. I wanted to speak up, but you can't be a superman here. It could cost you your life. There's nobody to report it to. Their bosses are just higher up in the corruption chain. The neighborhood I moved into is known as one of the most notorious in my city. It has a history going all the way back to the '80s. To be honest, every neighborhood here is dangerous.

I stay away from all that though. I have a job. I have my own apartment. And I have some friends. I even rescued a dog. I see Mexico as a fresh start for me. I have no history here. I'm starting from scratch. I will always miss the people and places I used to know. They're a part of who I am. But I need to live

---

1   Immigration Customs and Enforcement

in the present and look forward instead of back. We've got to survive and thrive no matter where we land. I'm just happy to be free.

Luis, who was deported after serving 10 years beginning at age 16, now lives in a large Mexican city where he works full-time as a call center agent for an internet company. He also provides translation services for Free Minds' Spanish-speaking book club. He is saving up to enroll in flight school. His dream is to become an international commercial pilot, flying routes across Europe, Asia, and the Middle East. He especially wants to visit Dubai.

Last Summer

by David

Sleepless nights and endless love

Distractions afar

The summer haze clouding the world around us

Discrete discussions

Fingers entwined and hearts sealed

Chasing dreams of quiet storms and warm winters

Looking into your emerald worlds

My fears ceased

A Familiar Soul

by Jonas

As soon as you meet one another
There's not even the shadow of a doubt
That the encounter was meant to be
It's as if the universe stops
Just for a moment
To acknowledge this union
And cast a warm smile upon
A small portion of destiny realized
And you both feel it in your core

Your eyes connect with one another
And instantly you feel this sense of peace,
Comfort, and safety
Flashes of intuition bring forth images
Of the two of you in your mind's eye

And you not only know this person
You know her intimately
You understand him deeply
And you know that the connection
That the two of you share
Is so deeply rooted in the cosmos
That this couldn't just be
A figment of your imagination

And as your eyes meet once again
You've never been more sure of
Anything else in your life

No te prometo

por Luis

No te prometo la luna
Ni todo el dinero del mundo
No te prometo otro mundo

No te prometo las estrellas
Ni el cielo, no te haré promesas falsas
No te diré cosas sin sentirlas

No te prometo la luna
Tal vez no pueda regalarte un paraíso
Por si mantendras en tu cara una sonrisa

No te prometo las estrellas
Tal vez no pueda regalarte dramantes
Pero mi amor por ti es verdadero

No te prometo la luna
Tal vez no pueda darte lujos pero mi Corazón es tuyo
Tal vez no puedo llevarte a lugares lujosos
Pero espero con mi amor poder conquistar tu Corazón

I Don't Promise You

by Luis

I don't promise you the moon
Nor all the money in the world
I don't promise you another world

I don't promise you the stars
Nor the sky, I won't give you false promises
I won't tell you things I don't feel

I don't promise you the moon
Maybe I can't give you paradise
But you will keep a smile on your face

I don't promise you the stars
Maybe I can't give you diamonds
But my love for you is true

I don't promise you the moon
Maybe I can't give you luxuries but my heart is yours
Maybe I can't take you to fancy places
But I hope with my love to conquer your heart

Caroline shares her perspective as the
girlfriend of someone who was incarcerated.

Caroline
(conversation)

When I first met him, my sister was like, "Caroline, are you crazy, what are you doing?" I'd never really dealt with a guy who had been in his situation as far as being incarcerated. I'm like, *he's not a bad guy.* You know, once you sit and you listen to someone's story and see where they're coming from. He's been through a lot of things that were unfortunate that really didn't have to happen to him that caused him to get locked up. He has a good head on his shoulders. He's very intelligent. And when he first started telling me about his poetry, I was, like, *Yeah, sure, you write poetry.* Because all these guys, they're, like, rapping and it's just talk. But he showed me some of his poems. So, I'm like, *Oh, you're seriously doing this.*

He even wrote some poetry for me while he was locked up. Because I was devastated. Because when I met him, we were like best friends. From the time I met him, we were together all the time. And we had got a place together. And then he got locked up, which kind of put the burden on me to take care of all the bills. Because I'm, like, *I'm not trying to lose this place.* He wrote me a poem called "Overwhelmed, Overwhelmed, Don't Be Overwhelmed." I would think about that when I would start feeling the pressure and getting sad. Because I couldn't call him, couldn't talk to him, couldn't see him, like I wanted to.

It was very hard. You had to go to the video visit center, right beside the jail. It's always video—you don't get to hug them, touch them, nothing, nope. No type of human contact. So

what do you do when your loved one is hurt and suffering? You can't even hug them. You come, sign in, and then sit at the computer station they tell you to sit at. And you wait for the screen to pop on and see his face on the screen and yours is up in the corner. Kind of like FaceTime. But you can't do it from your phone; you have to go there to do it.

Some days, it was tough getting up there. Because I didn't have a car at the time, I would catch the train. One day I got there, and they had cancelled the visit. They didn't give notice beforehand. I'm like, *I've come all this way. I've worked all day. I want to see him.* And they're just so nonchalantly, like, "It's cancelled." And then they look at you—because I'm upset—waiting for my reaction. Like amusement for them: *Is she going to yell, scream?* Because I've seen them do this to other people. So it's no reason for me to act crazy up in here and yell, scream, and curse at you. I was hurt, though. And of course, he's on the inside upset. Sometimes it's for stupid reasons. Or lockdown. I don't remember what it was that time. But I do remember being sad going home.

It made me feel like, you know, you shouldn't treat people this way. Do you have to be so mean to the incarcerated people? To the families? Is there a way that you could just treat them like human beings? I'm just here to see him. But you're treating me like I've committed a crime too. Like talking down to me. But, I'm like, he's in jail, so I guess this is what you have to go through.

He was sent to federal prison. They don't even tell you the day that they're going. It's just one day you go visit him, and he's gone. I went and they were, like, "Nah, he's gone to the feds." Kentucky. A lot of people find out that way. It was tough. I did put it in my GPS to find out how long it would take to drive to Kentucky. But it was ridiculous, like, 14, 15 hours. If it was just up to New York or something, I probably would have did it. Or even down south, maybe South Carolina, North Carolina. But I'm not familiar with that part of the country and don't want to do that by myself. So we would send pictures and would write.

In total, he was gone for three years. Most of the time I've known him, he's been in jail. But he's out this time, and he's doing better. He's happier than he was last time he was out. He was there for his son's graduation from high school. His daughter's from middle school. So he's very happy that he was able to be there for those events. Just seeing his kids on a regular basis, being able to call them and talk to them, makes him feel good. Not having the phone cut off or have someone bust in. I think sometimes they just need to allow the guys to have more of an outlet while they're in there. Don't take everything from them. You know, some of them are artists. Some of them like to draw. Some of them like music. Like, give them more of an outlet while they're in there so that they don't have time to mess with each other because they're frustrated.

I mean, I know it's jail, and they're serving time for a crime that they have committed. Supposedly. But don't treat them so bad. There's no respect or compassion. It makes you feel like you don't matter, you know? You have to have other people around you to build you up. Or incorporate more programs to help build the guys up. So for the guys to come out and be successful, I think they need some type of support group to help them. Whether it's something like Free Minds or some other type of group or whatever.

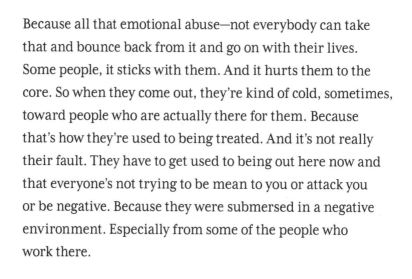

Because all that emotional abuse—not everybody can take that and bounce back from it and go on with their lives. Some people, it sticks with them. And it hurts them to the core. So when they come out, they're kind of cold, sometimes, toward people who are actually there for them. Because that's how they're used to being treated. And it's not really their fault. They have to get used to being out here now and that everyone's not trying to be mean to you or attack you or be negative. Because they were submersed in a negative environment. Especially from some of the people who work there.

I don't know if it's hard for the guards to do that to people. Or if they just get desensitized over the years. I don't know if they have a bad day at home and just come in and take it out. All of the guys are not bad. But the guards just see them that way. They just see all these guys in orange, and they're all the same to them. They don't see their faces. They don't see them for who they are. They're only a number. Sometimes they don't even know their name.

Tears

by Sylvester

If I was a tear in your eyes;

I would roll down your cheeks into your beautiful lips;

But if you were a tear in my eyes;

I would never cry because I would be afraid of losing you.

Even Hurricanes Make Flowers Grow

by Jean-Marc

I was a destroyer
A fickle force of nature
Who strolled through life
Damaging
Every soul I touched
Then you came into me
A storm
You ignited a conflagration
Within me
That catalyzed my transformation
Into the man you see before you
Fire burns
Not to destroy
But to transform
Transmute
Transmogrify
A change in temperament
Tempered by the slick touch
Of the woman who loves me
You have my hurricane
But even hurricanes make flowers grow

My Heart

by Derrick I.

My heart is so torn
Like a hand-me-down
I feel worn
My heart feels punctured
From a thick vine of thorns
My heart is caged
Sabotaged with rage
But can't break free
The only words for its freedom
Is hearing you say you love me
In my dreams you are all I see
So for that moment
Your presence brings peace to me
But when I wake
It's hard to face reality
It's hard to face the truth
My blood pressure is higher
Than a skyscraper roof
Stress having me feel like
Not knowing what to do
So I stress myself to sleep
To be with you

I KNOW PAIN

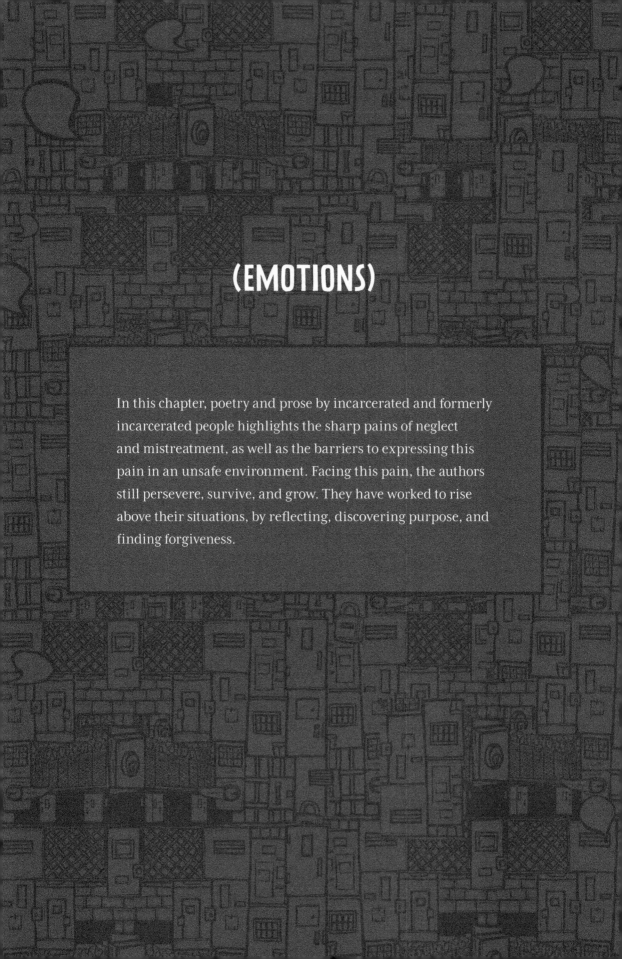

(EMOTIONS)

In this chapter, poetry and prose by incarcerated and formerly incarcerated people highlights the sharp pains of neglect and mistreatment, as well as the barriers to expressing this pain in an unsafe environment. Facing this pain, the authors still persevere, survive, and grow. They have worked to rise above their situations, by reflecting, discovering purpose, and finding forgiveness.

I Know Pain

by D'Angelo

I know pain like the back of my hand
I've felt it on my skin like wind from a fan
I've cradled it like a baby and rocked it to sleep
Spilled it all over my clothes and all over my sheets
I've loaded it into guns and forced others to accept it
I've harmonized with its voice and drove it in every direction
It walks when I walk and breathes when I breathe
Yeah I know pain and pain knows me
It mimics my behavior and dares me to get mad
It wants me, haunts me, and taunts me when I'm glad
It made its way into my life and won't let me be
Yeah I know pain and pain knows me

Nick
(conversation)

I was a foster kid. My mother had me when she was only 15. She just wasn't prepared to raise a child. Eventually, they made my mother bring me to the Child Protective Services building. I didn't know why I was there. But then I seen my mother getting on the elevator and the elevator door closing. I ran after her and started crying and calling out to her, and they all pulled me back. I remember just riding around to different houses that day because no one would take me. Finally, they found me a foster home. Yeah, that's how I got taken away.

They left me there at night with this lady. I woke up the next morning; I'm thinking I'm going to school. But she was like, "Nah you not going to school." I'm like, "Is my social worker coming back?" She just said, "No." I'm just in some strangers' house, I don't know none of them. I remember sitting there at the table eating my cereal and I just broke down crying. I couldn't eat my cereal anymore. I couldn't stop crying and you know, I guess she was just very irritated by me. She made me go up to my room for the rest of the day.

Things got worse. I knew I didn't belong there. They always was trying to make me feel like an outsider. They would go on family field trips, but they ain't never take me on the little trips they went on. And you know foster parents, they get money for the foster kids. But I didn't see no money. She didn't buy me no clothes or anything. I wore the same clothes for almost the whole year. It got so bad, they started calling me

"monkey," telling me I looked like a monkey, that ain't nobody wanted me, that's why I was there. That hurt my soul, deeply. Because that was actually the truth. Nobody didn't ever come and see me, nobody wanted me.

I was clumsy and I wasn't always a good kid. One time, I accidentally broke something small in the house and when I told my foster mother, she just started whooping me, punching me. It wasn't even anything she cared about. It was just an excuse to beat me.

Another day, my friend and I were playing on the school bus. We were throwing a battery back and forth at each other. I threw it and it accidentally hit my friend in the face and he got a black eye. I didn't mean to hurt him. The school bus had to stop and the police came, picked me up, and dropped me off at my foster home. They suspended me from school. My foster mother locked me in my bedroom with the lights out. I was there for hours and hours. Finally, I found a box of books in the room. I started reading Dr. Seuss books, Three Little Bears books. I be just sitting in the room reading all day in the dark. It was like a relief, an escape. I guess she eventually realized how quiet I was because she came up and took the books away from me. I was just locked in the dark, pacing back and forth just waiting for her to call me down to eat. Instead, she came up and beat me so bad that when it was time to go back to school, she wouldn't let me go because I was all bruised up and she didn't want the school to see.

I missed and thought about my mother every day. I loved her more than anything. All I wanted was to be able to go back home with her. One year in that foster home was worse than the 10 years I spent in prison.

Since I got home from prison, I've maintained a full-time job and started my own catering business. My mom and I have built a strong relationship. I have a beautiful young son. I got my high school diploma in prison and I will go to college. My dream is to one day build my catering business up and hire kids who've been in foster care, giving them job skills training and work experience. These kids are lonely and they feel like there is nobody out there who cares about them. I want to be that person who steps up to let them know I will be there.

I drove past my foster mother's house a couple of times. I wanted to knock on her door. If I could see my foster mother now, I don't know what I would say. I want her to know what I look like. How healthy I am and how good I'm doing now. It wouldn't be hate coming out of my mouth, but I would probably tell her about all of my accomplishments. I would show her that even with everything I went through, I still made it out good. I didn't let none of that break me down.

At the age of 17, Nick was sentenced to adult prison. He now works full-time as a community relations liaison. He is a devoted father to his young son. A published poet, Nick has also written *Watch Lil' Moe Go-Go*, a children's picture book celebrating the beauty and inclusivity of DC's official music.

Do Grown Men Cry?

by DeAngelo M.

All things, it seems to me, must we test

Accept the truth, reject the rest

So we must investigate or try to see what makes a grown man cry

Macho, big, tough, and strong

To admit their tears they think is wrong

But let me tell you on the sly

Yes!

These "real, grown" men do cry

Mom is gone now - that's very tough

Didn't hug her near enough

She's with her maker in the sky

Forgiveness causes a grown man to cry

Leave your homeland - perhaps forever

Start a new life - forget home never

You may in this new land die

Memories may cause a grown man to cry

Blanks filled in?

Now take a good look, what have you written in your life's book

If for reasons you come up dry...

That alone should cause your grown a** to cry...

Sometimes I Cry

by Delonte

I told a million lies, now it's time to tell a single truth

Sometimes I cry!

It's hard dealing with my pride, not knowing whether to fight or flee

Sometimes I cry!

Hard to maintain this image of a tough guy

When deep down inside I am terrified!

If I ever told you I wasn't scared, I lied

Struggling to make it back to society and my family

I cry!

I cry for my son, who I barely see

Due to these mountains

And me and his mom's beef

I cry for my siblings, who never knew their older brother

Because he stayed in the streets

I cry for my grandma, who is now deceased

I cry for my life, half of which they took from me

I cry for my anger and rage, the only emotions I can show in this place

I cry for how we treat each other inside these walls

I cry for the lack of unity we have, most of all!

When will it end, I want to know

Till then, all I can do is let these tears flow...

Delonte died of COVID-19 in May 2020.

Inside vs. Outside

by Linda

While looking at my face you would think, "Oh, she's pretty." You would never think she would get locked up, that she knows how it feels to be hurt. Though, inside you would notice my heart is my window to my past. The pain I dealt with, the beatings I took, when I was younger. You would notice my heart has a hole in it where all the good times fall into and you notice everything is around it. Outside you would see a face that smiles, but on the inside, I'm crying. I cry for the little girl trapped inside who couldn't cry when she was younger. Inside I cry so much that no one really knows the true me. Outside I act strong and as if nothing could hurt me. I'm tired of crying on the inside! Crying on the outside, people notice not everything is peaches-n-cream.

Cheleta
(conversation)

A lot of us '80s babies lost our parents at an early age. My father was a bank robber. I was five years old when he got sentenced to 10 years at Lorton.[1] My mom started using crack. She didn't die back then, but we lost her. She sometimes came around for birthdays and holidays.

My grandmother took us in. I was an ambitious child. I was an honor roll student and a standout athlete. I was a bright star. Everyone who seen me, they just knew I was going to go far. But I was being abused inside the home. My grandmother seen me as a demon. She beat all of us, but she used to call me the devil. I been beat with switches, cable cords, fists, irons, frying pans, bats. Anything that can be used as a weapon, I been hit with it. Once she stabbed me in the neck with a screwdriver. When I was eight years old, one of my grandmother's boyfriends raped me. When I told her, she didn't believe me. I would run away, but the police always brought me right back home.

I became very rebellious. I started fighting back. I just wanted my mother. It was a yearning. When I was 14, I left to live with her in abandoned houses. I took cold baths and watched my mother on crack.

I remember I once asked my grandmother, "Why do you hate me?" Her response was, "Because I see your mother in you—

---

1   Lorton Reformatory served as the District of Columbia's prison until it closed in 2001.

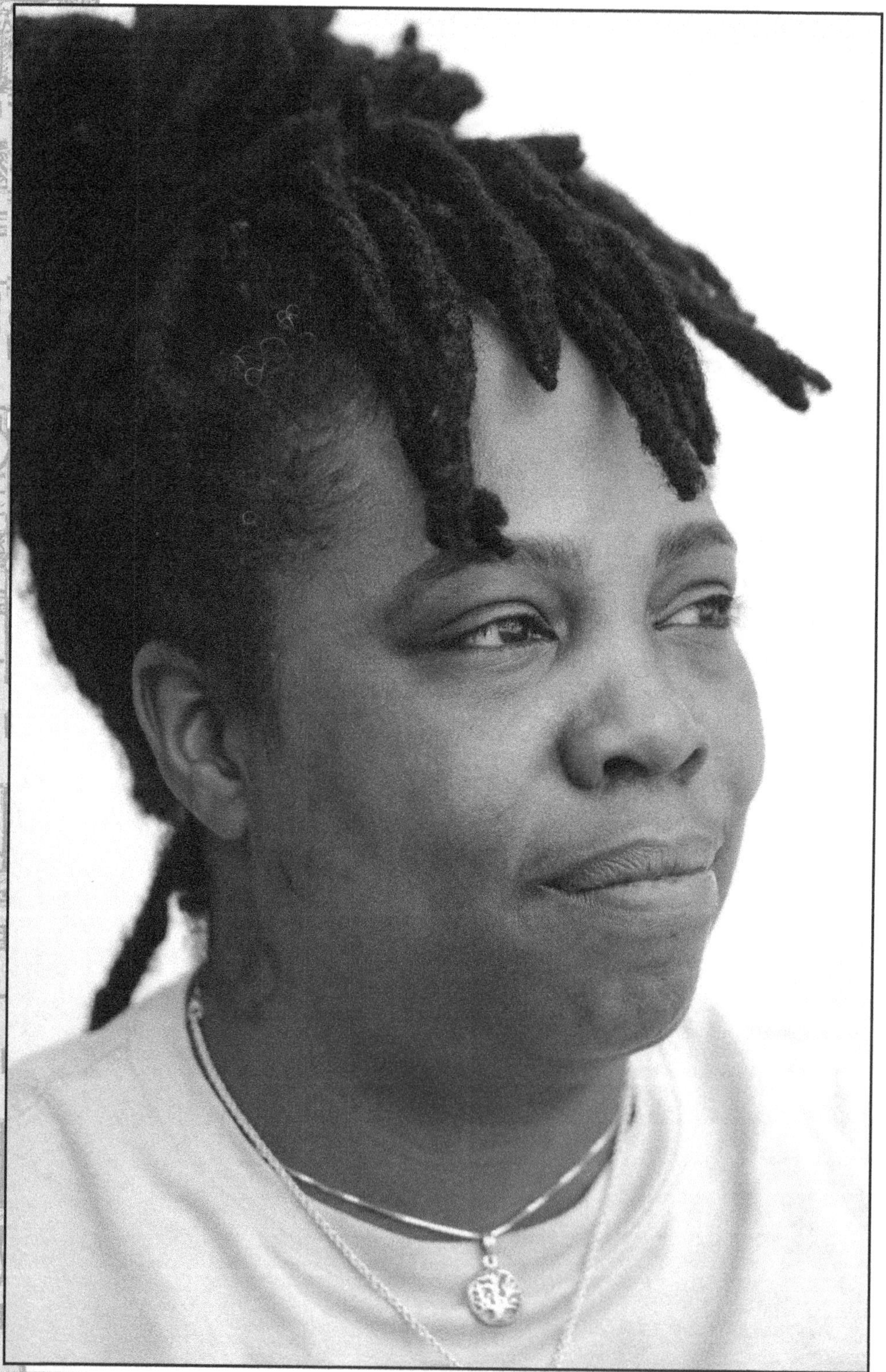

the good and the bad. And I don't want to lose you to crack too." The thing is, she never gave me a chance. It wasn't right, but it was out of fear.

By this time, I was just wild. I walked around school with a gun on me. I had a backpack, but wasn't no books in it. I was just living to die. I was a senior in high school when I was arrested for armed robbery. I got sentenced to eight years. I just snapped. I went crazy. I fought wardens, I set fires. I was fighting and inciting riots. I didn't see anything wrong with the things I was doing. I felt people owed me something inside of prison. But they didn't owe me nothing. They didn't put me behind bars. I did.

About eight months into my bid, I was beaten up real bad by officers. They kicked me in my face. I was rushed to the hospital with fractured ribs and a fractured jaw. Somehow my family heard about it and called the prison. They thought I was dead. When I talked to my grandmother, she told me, "I don't want you to die in there, Cheleta. Please just come home!" I think that day scared my grandmother.

Our relationship changed after that. She would send me money here and there. My grandmother didn't know how to read and write. I knew there would never be a response back, but I would write to let her know I was thinking about her. She never apologized for what she did. My grandmother went through a lot of physical abuse and neglect herself. It took me a long time—years—but I have forgiven her. I had to face a lot of unhealed wounds. My grandmother did what she did because of her own trauma.

The crazy thing? In the midst of all of this—going in and out of the SHU,[2] constantly being under investigation, and getting transferred—I applied myself to the stuff I wanted to do. I got all kind of certificates, including HVAC. I can take an air conditioner apart and rebuild it myself. I learn fast, and I'm hella smart. My teacher pushed me to take the GED. I was in the SHU when they came to tell me I passed. They let me out of solitary just for that day to attend the graduation celebration. My friends were all there. It was overwhelming. Everyone was hollering for me. It felt good.

I read a book in the SHU called *The Making of a Slave.* It's a speech made back in the 1700s by a slaveholder named Willie Lynch, telling white people how to make slaves be obedient. That book changed the way I thought. He wrote about the "slave mentality" which is to obey and follow. I realized I had a slave mentality. I'd been obeying and following what everyone else around me was doing. Using PCP, drinking, wanting the latest Jordan's and pockets fat with money. I was an idiot. I was ambitious and intelligent, but I was an idiot because I allowed who I truly was to be hidden. I had so much to offer but my slave mentality took that away from me. Reading that book was an *aha!* moment for me.

I grew up in prison. The older women guided and tried to protect me. I called them OT's, for "old timers," but they were like aunties. I think the experience of incarceration is different for women. There are more bonds with us. We are more emotional. We need something and someone. Women in prison provide that to each other. We also experience a different type of hardship. I've seen so many mothers crying after visits with their kids. Or they haven't seen their child.

---

2   Secure Housing Unit, also known as solitary confinement

They sitting there reading the letters, shaking and crying.
They just want to touch their child. The hardest day in prison,
every year, is Mother's Day. It's an eerie feeling.

I don't think the justice system is adequately designed to meet
the needs of women. There are way less programs provided
for women—in prison, and also in reentry. There is an extra
stigma in our society for women convicted of crimes. People
still expect women to be soft and submissive. They don't
understand a woman committing a crime or being in prison.
It's not feminine. When people find out I've been incarcerated,
they start treating me like I'm hard. They don't see me as a
woman anymore. I become something else.

Who am I now? I've changed. I am a person with emotions
now. Someone who actually cares about living. I value my
life. I value my partner, my friends and my family. I didn't
used to feel like I had anything to live for. But now I do. I want
to go as far as I can go in my career, to travel the world as a
motivational speaker, and to work with at-risk kids. I'll share
my story with them, show them that I was once where they sit
now. You gonna remember this story. I'm gonna be somebody
very important!

The day I was released was an awesome day. As I was leaving,
a bunch of the officers said, "We'll see you when you come
back." I told them, "I ain't never coming back. They'll bury me
first!" As soon as I got to DC, I went to see my grandmother.
It was the first stop I made. She cooked me the whole meal
that I asked for: potato salad, fried chicken, chitlins and some
greens. She made everything I asked for, and we ate together.

Cheleta is a published poet. She works full-time as a mail handler with the US Postal Service. As one of the founding members of The WIRE (Women Involved in Reentry Efforts), Cheleta's passion is to provide social support and life skills training to women in prison who are dealing with anger issues as a result of trauma. She speaks on justice issues at conferences across the country.

Mirror

by DeVonte

Forever seemed like never

Until pain found my doorstep

Some lines I leave lingering

Because I never want you to think less

Life is so impressive once you inherit this perception

Forced in different directions

But in every field I've been accepted

Maybe because my soul stayed pure

Or my differences from the rest I never let interfere

I hung love in the closet and put happiness on my back

Hid pain in a place I'll never want to go to get it back

Address me right and your letter should reach its destination

I know workers with no occupations

And every second that's been invested

Has been self destructive in various places

A dazed boxer was saved by a bell

A suicidal man was saved by religion

A lady that gave up on her dreams was saved by a vision

Now imagine you on the edge of that cliff

What's going to save you from what's tempting?

True Feelings
by Muquan

Sometimes it feels like unspoken words carry the greatest sorrow
Weeping night after night praying for a break tomorrow
My heart carries a burden that shows on my face
I feel confused and out of place
So I use this pen to show me the way
As I write these words my eyes they shower
Lost and afraid, in my darkest hour

Born Invisible

by Alazajuan

So what's next, I guess continue to be used like Windex
I live life invisible
So people don't see my hurt and pain
I'm so invisible, I'm clear as a cloud
And see-through like rain
So invisible, I'm the rocks underneath
The snow on a mountain in Maine
Why be seen if I'm going to be overlooked
Thrown to the side and misjudged
Like a cover of a book
Or just hang me out to dry like a clothesline hook
Once again my tears evaporate on the breeze
Then cast away into the sea
A cycle that put my heart at ease
I was born invisible
But who really gives a care?
Blending in with the dark is no longer a fear
It's a burden I've become able to bear
Hope one day I can be bright, like lights
In Times Square
Born invisible.

Listener

by Davon W.

There are things I can't tell my mother
So I come to you
I'll never tell my human friends
'Cause they don't listen as well as you do
The way you listen
Is like a kid with his ear to a seashell
You hear everything I say
And the echo as well
I like the way you hold your water
And keep my secrets in your head
Paper, that's why you're the best listener
'Cause you never repeat what I said

Violence

by Brandon

Oh Violence, why have you come to destroy me?

What womb of a woman can conceive such a hideous person?

Your face is like a shadow

Dark with indescribable features

Your scent of blood draws me closer to death

You show up when there's a crowd

You love to see and hear confusion

I know when you're around

Because everything starts to move in slow motion

My ears become silent and I could feel my heart beat faster

You influence me to harm my people

You tell me that I'll be victorious against my enemies

But in the end, all I have managed to do was shed innocent blood

You have caused my family to disown me

When my family sleeps through the night

They are hunted by dreadful memories of me

Oh Violence, I wish to see you no more

I will defeat you with prayer

I'll overpower you once and for all

Goodbye, Violence

TAKIN' LOSSES

(GRIEF)

This chapter explores the magnitude of loss, from gun violence to family tragedies. A victim of violent crime shares her perspective on the justice system and her experience of loss alongside the experiences of incarcerated and formerly incarcerated writers. Their stories overlap and diverge in ways that illustrate how the absence of space to cope with these losses, and the lack of a support system, prevents healing and closure.

Eight Years Ago

by Will

Eight years ago, you told me we will be okay
As we sat on the steps contemplating that day
That day in which poverty wouldn't be a problem
That day where bullets and colors are not a trend

Eight years ago, you told me you wanted in
I asked why, you said to be homies 'til the end
Family was missing and money was needed
Life didn't play fair so revenge became a remedy

Eight years ago, you told me you needed a friend
To dismiss all sadness within
Since then, you became a brother to me
I would take a bullet for you and you for me

Eight years ago, the streets was all I knew
Without emotions I carried through
Looking for death around each corner
I was shot and you was told by a spectator

Eight years ago, you saw me in pain
I told you I would take care of it when the time came
That would be our last exchange of words
The last time I would see my brother

Eight years ago, I lost a good friend
Because of bullets that should have claimed me, he sought revenge
Stabbed more than eighteen times, his last goodbye
Was steps away from the steps where he said everything will be okay

Eight years ago, I should have prayed
Prayed for forgiveness instead of hatred
Prayed for another chance at sanity
Instead, all I saw were many tragedies

Ebonee
(conversation)

I grew up in the Trinidad neighborhood of Washington, DC. I had a curfew, but I didn't always stick to it. I didn't worry about violence back then. I knew young people who got locked up, but I never knew anyone who got shot. I don't know why it's so different now. When I was growing up, I never had to deal with none of this. Maybe fights, getting jumped, but never dealing with gun violence.

I have seven children between the ages of 10 and 20 years old. It's a busy household. We laugh and joke all the time. We do Tik Toks or play video games together. We just have a lot of fun together.

Everything changed in 2019. It was about 7:30 on Valentine's day. We were in our house watching TV and Roy'Ale (who was 12 then) asked can he go to the store. I was like, *Yeah, you can go to the store but come right back.* He was like, *Ma, you know I always come right back.* Wasn't long after he went out the door, all we heard was a bunch of gunshots. Now at that particular time in 2019, we heard gunshots frequently. But I knew he had just gone out the door, so I went outside riding around trying to find him and couldn't find him. Then I see somebody laying on the ground. It was Roy'Ale. I jumped out the car and said, *That's my son!* When I got to him, he wasn't breathing. He got shot in the back and the bullet came out through the top part of his chest. The bullet missed his spine and his heart by a half inch, but it collapsed his left lung and fractured three of his ribs. He was in the hospital for 22 days...11 of those were spent in ICU.

Ebonee shares her perspective as the
mother of two sons injured by gun violence.

When my son got home, he was different. He hates loud sounds now. He doesn't like the 4th of July. He doesn't want to go outside anymore and when he does, he wears a hood on his head. Roy'Ale's brother Roy'Nal is just a year older than him. The two of them are really close. After his brother got shot, he always made sure Roy'Ale was comfortable and felt safe. He knew that his little brother didn't want to be out after the sun went down.

It was in May, less than three months later, I was on my way home from work when I got a call from my daughter. She told me that Roy'Nal got shot. I couldn't believe it. I was just numb. Roy'Nal was outside waiting for me to get home from work that night so he could go to the grocery store with me. It was one of his favorite things we did together. He had just gotten off his bike and was standing there speaking to his friends. That's when a person stood on the sidewalk and just started shooting at them. Roy'Nal was the only one that got hit. He's now paralyzed from the waist down.

There's a different feel in our family now. I can't describe it. I still have both of my sons here, but I still lost something. We all did. Not that we're sad and hurt all the time. We all still have fun together—we laugh and we joke and we still play, but everything changed in a matter of seconds. Literally everything for our family is different from what it used to be. If we want to go anyplace, it takes longer than it used to because now my son is paralyzed. He needs time to get dressed and get in the car. We have to plan around all of that. It used to be we could just get up and go. We can't do that anymore. My other son, he only wants to stay in the house. It went from, *Yeah, let's go!* to *Nah, I don't know if I really want to go...Who going? How long we gonna be there?* It's hard to feel carefree now.

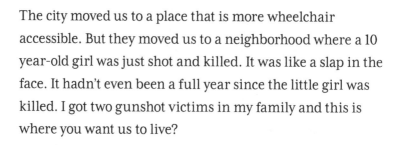

The city moved us to a place that is more wheelchair accessible. But they moved us to a neighborhood where a 10 year-old girl was just shot and killed. It was like a slap in the face. It hadn't even been a full year since the little girl was killed. I got two gunshot victims in my family and this is where you want us to live?

Nobody has been arrested in either of my sons' cases. The police don't think the shootings are related and they say my sons weren't intended targets. A lot of people have told me my sons were just in the wrong place at the wrong time. That makes me mad. Because how you at the wrong place when you just going home? How's it the wrong time when it's 7:30 on Valentine's Day? Or 9:30 in the summertime when the sun just went down. How is that the wrong place and the wrong time?

I don't feel like enough has been done to solve these cases. It's not a high priority anymore. If no one comes forward with new information, they're not investigating it. A lot of people know what happened to both of my sons, but no one is speaking up and telling the police what they saw.

I feel like the justice system could work if more people would speak out on the things that they see. How can the system work if nobody says anything? Unfortunately, everybody believes in the "no-snitch" culture. At one point, I went to school to become a probation and parole officer. One of my teachers broke down the definition of snitching to us. She said if you speak of the things you saw, that's not snitching. But if you with a person and y'all both commit a crime, and you tell on the other person, *that's* snitching. Like, if I saw a man break in to this blue car, I'm not snitching. I'm telling what I

saw. But if I'm an accomplice to the person that's breaking into the blue car, and I go and tell, that's snitching. I wish people understood the difference.

I think about the people who did this every single day. Especially when I see my son in the chair. I'm glad and I'm blessed that he is still here, but when I see him in the chair, and when I see Roy'Ale with his shirt off and he got the scars and marks, it reminds me what happened to them. I can't forget it. I want to know why. I'm over the hurt phase. Now, it's mostly anger. I just want to know why. Why you shoot my sons?

If I could talk to the people who shot them, I would tell them about the hell they put me and my family through. The emotional and physical scars. The fact that they don't feel safe no more. Not just my sons, but all of us are dealing with the scars from what was done to them.

I'll be honest, I want the people who did this to feel what my sons went through. I want the person that shot my son to know how it feels to be paralyzed from the waist down. To know what it is to one second have just gotten off a bike and now you wheelchair-bound. I want you to have the scars that he has. Not just physical but mental. I want them to feel what they made my sons feel.

I don't think I've really dealt with what happened. I really haven't. I put all my energy into taking care of my family. And that means I had to push resentment and hate for the people who did this to the side. I had to be able to do that for my family. And to tell the truth, I don't know how we can balance punishing people who commit crimes with preparing them to

return to the community and live differently. I just really don't know. It's too personal for me.

I do know that I want to see a good thing come out of what happened to my sons and my family. I started participating in anti-gun violence initiatives. After my second son got shot, I helped organize a peace walk. It felt good because I had people behind me and we were all saying the same thing: *Stop gun violence and increase the peace!* It made me feel good that even people not from this neighborhood were marching right along with us. I feel like it made people pay attention. Because if you notice, they always do things for people who pass away from gun violence, but they never do things for people who actually survive. On the anniversary of my sons' shootings, we celebrate. We're not marking the day that they got shot, but we're celebrating the fact that they survived that day.

I do everything I can to take care of my kids and support their dreams. Roy'Nal is a rapper. He and his siblings are making songs and videos. Roy'Nal thought because he was in a wheelchair he couldn't go bowling again. I took them all bowling, and out of all of us, he ended up winning! I took him skating, even though he thought it was kind of weird, him having skates on and I'm pushing him around the skating rink. He still goes to Six Flags all the time. He's got a clothing line he's working on. And he goes into the studio. I just try to help them focus on their dreams the best way that I can.

If I could give just one message to any young person, it would be this: *Don't let a 10-second decision ruin the rest of your life and the lives of others.* I look at things differently now. I see how these kids are dying and I know I'm blessed to still have mine alive. This motivates me to speak out more.

Dear Mom

by Tariq

Tariq's mother was killed on 9/11/2001 in the attack on the World Trade Center

Mom,
Even though it's been over 19 years
Since that tragic day
It's still difficult finding the right words
To express what I'd like to say
I don't sit and dwell on the what ifs
Or what will never be
I busy myself giving thanks
For the precious moments you shared with me
I haven't always made the kinds of choices
That would make you proud of me
But I'd like you to know I've dedicated myself
To becoming the man you raised me to be
The pain I felt on that clear day in September
Is one that will stay with me
One I'll always remember
I'm all cried out
Tears no longer fall from my eyes
I love you, I miss you
Until we meet again
My heart forever cries

A Letter to Amari (My Little Brother)

by Mauda'Rico

It was kind of hard looking you into your eyes
Now that I look back on the past
And telling you I would always be around to have your back
When the good times turned into bad
I'm daydreaming of the times you did a lot of wild stuff
And the times you made me mad
Now all I do is reminisce about them same moments
And just smile and laugh, LOL

I remember asking you, "Why you're in these streets? What is it you trying
    to do or get?"
You said, "Shoes, clothes and females," and then asked me what about me?
And I said, "I'm tryin' to get rich, and the rest going to follow me."
Then life split us up, so we had no choice but to go our separate ways
So my broken promises you could never cope with
Chasing dreams, females and money became your thing
Then all of you began to fade away

That's when one day I called home and what I heard crushed my soul and
    took my spirit
Right then I had to whisper in your ear,
"I love you little brah and miss you, and when I go home I got you
I promise to do what's right!"
But this time I don't get a smart mouth or a, "I'm coolin' brah," and, "Ima
    be aite."
It was just silent, no noise, no comments, no nothing
Just plain and simple silence
So I have to cope with your broken promise to never fall victim to these streets
Your broken promise to move in silence and watch your back

Your promise to always be there for your daughters, SMH

Today there are no winners, just broken promises with no beginnings
The streets were never our friend because after all this, the streets are still
    there!
I love you brah and tell Dre, Day-Day, and Mello
I sent my love with you
You don't have to worry about your twins or that situation that was left undid
"Rest In Peace," cause my word as a man, Ima get you!!!

Love 4 Life,
Rico

Takin' Losses
by Shawndell

I went from plentiful to pitiful, in a landslide

Took a face plant, nose dive; that hurt pride

Fell down so hard, now I won't climb

Or dust myself off and get on for another ride

'Cause I'm tryin' to heal from these bitter wounds

These trouble scars, I'm startin' to get used to

'Cause I suffer in silence

Tucked away in my own temporary place

As I drink away my liquid tears in private

It only hurts worse, when I try to smile on the surface

The what-it-seems, is not what-it-seems

Wishin' this was all a dream

That I can wake up and be free

Taste the fresh air, in a breeze

Feel life in grass and growth in trees

Then spread my eagle wings and

Let sun rays touch me

And never look back on these difficult days

Where nothing was given and all was taken

A journey so long, I got lost along the way

I've felt these suffocating hands of heartache

Squeeze me to bending knees

Until I threw up my hands in surrender

Praying for redemption, like I was the worst of sinners

Hopin' that I lose my mind and don't remember

All those agonies that was grabbing me

How I was unraveling and battling every

Conscience demon I've ever seen

Losing myself gradually

When I fell on hard luck

Knocked senseless when I was love struck

Everything swept from beneath me

Left with a hard heart and cold feet

All I hear is lies, I don't trust easy

Those eyes of reality I can't meet

'Cause there's a void in my soul

I've taken a loss of everything I've ever known

I'm scared to death to let go

But, I must face this inner fear

I gotta start somewhere

Like from the bottom and begin again

Or picking up where I fell off

But, this time, I'm protecting myself at all costs

From takin' another tragic loss

Gone Before I Knew It

by JoeNathan

I abandoned my community and stepped outside of my family

All 'cause the government thinks I had something to do with my situation

Gone before I knew it!

When I got hit by a car for the second time

In my head I was thinking, "That's the end!"

Until I felt my body jerk

Then I tried to get back up and that failed

So I stayed there…

Gone before I knew it

When me and one of my friends got into a car accident

I almost died 'cause I don't like seatbelts

Then when we hit the biggest tree on the block face up

I d*mn near went out the window face-first

Until my elbow hit the glass and stopped my crossing

Gone before I knew it

When I gave her that first kiss

I didn't know what to think or do next

So I just went home and rested on it

Gone before I knew it

The first day I started smoking weed

I went to a whole new state of mind that we call "Cloud Nine"

I felt like I had the ability of physically ejecting my soul from my body

Some people out here getting so high off of poison

Somebody can stick a knife in them and they won't feel it

You're gone according to whatever someone gave you

Or someone said to you

Come back so we can love and fix you

Gone!

Eyone
(conversation)

I started losing people when I was six. That's how old I was when my grandmother died. My mother was just a teenager when she got pregnant with me. She and her sister looked after me, but it was my grandmother who raised me. She was the backbone of our family. She died of cancer. I cried and I was so hurt. Just a couple of months later, my mother died of a heroin overdose. Back to back. They took me to see my father in prison, so he could break the news to me about my mother. I once found a letter my father wrote at the time. He said, "Man, I'm worried about Eyone. He didn't even cry." But I was still crying out for my grandmother and I think losing them so close together, it created some kind of problem in me. No death was ever the same to me after that. The deaths I experienced later on in the streets was nothing compared to that. My heart was already cold.

My aunt left college and basically raised me until I was 16. All those years, I didn't want for anything. There wasn't extra, but the necessities were there. I started getting into trouble around 12. I got mean and rough and tough in the streets. I had uncles who were very important in the street culture. So I was aware of the violence and death. Older guys I knew were dying all around me.

My aunt saw what was coming. She sat me down and told me not to get involved. But it felt like I couldn't really help it. Violence started coming to us, and we started responding. Gun violence to be exact. I got to hanging with a group of guys

161

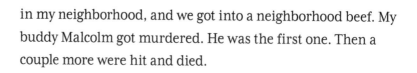

in my neighborhood, and we got into a neighborhood beef. My buddy Malcolm got murdered. He was the first one. Then a couple more were hit and died.

I was 16 when I was arrested and went to jail. A year after I got there, my cousin that I was raised with was stabbed to death. He was only 19. He was like a brother to me. I don't have siblings, so my cousins were my brothers and sisters. I cried, and I vowed to avenge his death. My mind was so different at that time in my life, I didn't know how to deal with loss. After my cousin got murdered, someone stabbed me in my neck while my back was turned. Not long after that a buddy was killed. All these things made me mean and mad. It did something to me. I had a life sentence at the time, so I wasn't nobody you play with.

Becoming a Muslim made me change. I submitted to something that came with discipline. When you a gangster, you think you rough and tough. Your rules are the rules and you make 'em up as you go. But when you accept and become a part of something that has a whole body of rules, there's almost a freedom in it. The decisions are made for me by this way of life. I do what's right at every corner. I don't have a decision—*Do I steal this or not?* Because the rules say you don't steal it. I grew and I learned that just because of what I went through in the world, or the cards I was dealt, didn't mean I had to make everyone else's life that I encountered a living hell.

In prison, I'd be on the phone with someone at home and that's how I'd find out someone was killed. I saw a lot of people getting that kind of news on the phone. We were hundreds, sometimes thousands of miles away from home. Visits were scarce. So you heard about deaths on the phone. One of the

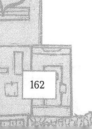

most painful parts was not being able to go to the funeral and be a part of that closure. You haven't seen a person and then they're dead and you know you're not going to see them again. And it's just over.

I don't think there is any way not to get numb. That's all you can do. When you experience something over and over again, it's human nature to get numb to it. That street violence will beat you up bad.

Loss has shaped me. I understand that nothing here lasts forever. I don't think people understand that life is short. People say that they understand. But they don't honor relationships the way you should. I know people who will stop speaking to their mother, stop speaking to their father. I honor my relationships. I don't ever stop speaking to people I care about. My connections are for life. If I meet you, and we're cool, then I'm gonna like you, if not love you, for the rest of my life. I take time seriously. I don't play with time because so much time has been taken.

The best way I know how to memorialize the people I've lost is through my writing. One of the perks of being a writer, is that writing is eternal. Even if your writing disappears, someone can remember or quote what you wrote for infinity. The people I've lost, I write about them.

Since I came home, I've felt called to be a part of stopping the violence. A few years ago, I was hired by the city to work with youth. The work that I get paid for now, I was already doing it in the neighborhood. I was already out there talking to kids. I don't do a whole lot of talking about what you should do, or what you shouldn't do. I can only tell them about what I've

done. I can share my story and my experience. I tell them about the people I have lost. I tell them it's too many to name. And the number is still climbing.

Eyone was incarcerated as an adult at the age of 17 and served 17 years in prison before being released in 2010. He is the author of 12 books. He works as a transformative mentor and violence prevention specialist with Youth Advocate Programs, Inc. He is a prisoners' rights and juvenile justice advocate, and a writing coach for Free Minds.

Homie from the Struggle

by Joe

Dedicated to Darius after he was killed by gun violence

Homie I remember as little kids we played Pop Warner football together. I remember losing and winning together.

Homie I remember the times we were at Ballou skipping class and going to the gym smoking weed together.

Homie I remember when I use to come around your way and we would talk about a lot of ways we can get some money together.

Homie I remember when we were both Title 16[1] and serving hard time over DC jail juvie block together. I remember when you asked the CO[2] can we be cellmates.

Homie I remember the long days and nights in our cell praying over our cases. I remember when we got bad news about our cases, and it was a lot of crying and punching the walls with sad faces.

Homie I remember when we use to be in competition with each other, you always beat me with the push-ups and I beat you with the pull-ups. We were a strong duo homie.

Homie I remember when you beat your case and you didn't return back to the unit. I was so happy with the news the CO brought to me. Plus all your commissary you left behind for me.

---

1   Title 16 refers to the DC code that states that juveniles can be charged as adults.
2   Correctional Officer

Homie this is the struggle we were born in. Our environment was designed for us to fail.

WE WERE MORE THAN HOMIES FROM THE STRUGGLE. WE WERE BROTHERS FROM THE STRUGGLE. LOVE YOU BROTHER!

I Wish

by James

Trees lose leaves, kids lose teeth
A stain on a white-t can be removed with bleach

Break a nail it'll grow again, Tylenol can ease the pain
Umbrellas can block da rain, you can replay a song to sing

Memories are priceless, temporarily uniting
Staring off into the distance, your face on the horizon

If I had 3 wishes, I'd stutter to make it clear
I wish...I wish...I wish you were here

I FORGIVE ME

(TRANSFORMATION)

The writers reflect on forgiveness and self-acceptance in this chapter in order to embrace healing, hope, and a new self-identity. A teacher contributes his perspective and history, illuminating the way the legal system views formal education as a marker of a person's worth. The writers in this section speak on transformation, aware of the way change is often portrayed as a choice between good and bad, and holding space for the nuances and the people who don't have the opportunities to make choices like this.

I Quit

by Demitrich

I told her one too many times
I quit smoking
She told me, "You lying," I tell her, "Trust me"
But deep down, I know 100%
That I won't quit
I told her at least 10 times I won't cheat
But I sat there and lied through my teeth
I wish I could've quit lying to her, but I
Never had the strength to do it, but now
It's too late, I quit quitting on
All the good stuff

The Lead

by Terrell

I thought I was leading the path to be all I can be
But along my journey, something was calling me
Pinching me and poking at my skin
I turned around and looked over my shoulder
And seen it was the streets calling me over
Slowly taking me off track from what I believe
And had me questioning my ability to *LEAD*
Everyone that followed went astray
Because they seen I started to go a different way
Seeing me sink was something they couldn't stand
So my people helped me up by lending me a hand

Jordan
(conversation)

I grew up in a DC neighborhood known as a "red zone" because of the high crime rate. It was survival of the fittest, really. My dad passed away to lung cancer when I was five years old. After that, it was just me, my mother, and my older brother. My mother had to be both mother and father, and that was stressful on her. She did the best she could and she kept it together for us. When I was still really little, my big brother would come home and my mother would sit me at the dinner table with them while they worked on his homework assignments. That really made an impression on me. It showed me that education mattered.

From the time I started kindergarten, I knew I wanted to go to college and become a businessman. I pictured myself walking down the street in a suit and tie, with my briefcase. That was my vision! I always loved school. I loved reading and writing, and I worked hard. It would hurt my soul when I knew a classmate got a higher grade on their test. So I would strive to be better, not necessarily better than them, but to be a better me and improve my own score.

In high school, I had an English teacher named Ms. Payne. Everybody thought Ms. Payne was the strictest, meanest teacher they ever met. I saw her differently though. She gave us constructive criticism—sometimes even *harsh* criticism. But when she told me that she knew I could write better, it lit a fire in me. I could tell Ms. Payne wanted me to succeed. She was a blessing in my life.

It was the things that I did outside of school that got me in trouble. My community lacked resources. We didn't even have a recreation center. If I wanted to go to the nearest rec center, I would have to go into a neighborhood that we didn't get along with—put myself in danger, just to go to a rec center. Our school was run down and underfunded. We had sports, but for someone who wasn't interested in joining the football or basketball team, there just wasn't anything else for us. So we were just in the streets. At 16, I was angry and frustrated. I was mature and intelligent, but there was nothing for me. Once school was over, there was no place for me to go to pour my talents into something. If I'd had that in my teenage years, it would have saved me.

I got arrested and charged as an adult for armed robbery of a store during my senior year. I had so much ahead of me— prom, graduation. I already had several college scholarship offers. I wanted more than anything for my mom and my grandmother to see me do all that. But in the heat of the moment, when you're 16, you don't think. I didn't even understand what I'd done until I had the chance to reflect. Unfortunately, my time to reflect came when I was sitting in an adult jail. I felt like my life was over.

Calling my mother from jail was the most heartbreaking call I have ever made. I knew how badly I'd let her down. She told me she loved me, but the emotion I felt hit me hard. I never wanted to feel that way again. I became severely depressed and started losing a lot of weight. Going to court was scary. The first number I heard was "five." Five years in prison. Ultimately, I was given a plea agreement and released on probation as long as I attended college. I got out because the judge believed in me. He believed I would go to college and succeed. I realized

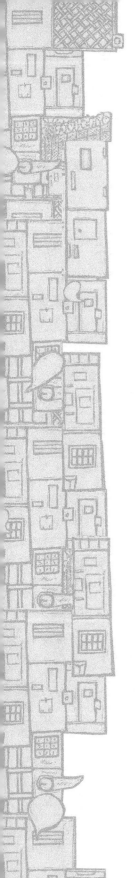

how much I had to be thankful for and promised myself I would do whatever it took to turn myself around.

I couldn't wait to get out of DC. I've been in DC all my life and I've seen more bad than good—witnessing shootings and things like that. But when I got to college, everyone I saw was going to class, or going to work. Everybody had a purpose. Being in a new atmosphere like this helped me to grow. I remember, I got to campus the weekend before classes. None of my roommates had arrived yet and I spent the whole weekend by myself. I was definitely nervous. I've always been an introvert. I didn't tell my roommates about my time in jail right away. But when I did start to open up, they were really supportive. They understood the obstacles that I overcame.

Pretty much every day, it still hits me: *Wow, I'm actually a college student!* It makes me feel proud when I tell people I go to college. I love it. I especially love all of my business classes. I can tell they are preparing me for the outside world. I feel lucky. There are a lot of DC kids who are really smart and they should be here too. I wish I could bring them along with me, to help them see that there is so much more for them. It hasn't been easy for me. Money has been a struggle. At one point, I wasn't sure if this would even happen. I came here for a reason though, and I'm not going to let anyone down. I won't ever give up.

After being sentenced in the adult system at the age of 17, Jordan is now a sophomore in college, studying business entrepreneurship. He also serves as a Poet Ambassador for Free Minds' violence prevention initiative, *On the Same Page*, sharing his story with youth across the city. He has testified numerous times in front of the DC Council to advocate for a more equitable and humane legal system. Jordan plans to start his own business after he graduates—possibly a clothing and sneakers shop—as well as continue to advocate for DC youth.

Standing

by JJ

I'm standing on the edge of a precipice

If I lose, I'm facing multiple celebrations behind locked doors

I'd miss seeing my nephews and cousins

Running around, playing together

Seeing them grow up to be successful

Missing their first heartbreak

Or their first fight

As I look down, I see the edge of the ocean

I feel like I'm holding a boulder

If I fall, I will sink

If I don't fall, I can throw the boulder off the cliff

And I will feel 7,000 pounds lighter

I will feel free

Because even if I fall

I can swim

Under Any Conditions
by Hosea

I graduated to the DC Jail
But my writing still excelled

Not letting nothing stop my growth
I read every book and wrote down every quote

In the dark by the window was the only light at night
I stayed in that same spot
For so many hours, that's where they flashed their light

In the cold with no blanket
It was things I had to put on paper, I couldn't fake it

I grew up from reading books
Opening my horizon
That life is bigger than what I see
These white walls and yards with no trees

Writing was like a fresh piece of toast
Writing was like my Holy Ghost

Old Scars, New Wound?

by Rico

The very moment I ask myself

Why do I feel this way?

There's this voice I continue to hear

And it says

Can we share?

In the moment, I answered back

Is something there?

Listen, bro, I know you as Rico

But the tendered heart, there were no one's hands there to shake

My personal vision, alone

I wanted to find a new home

So I reached out without a doubt

Someone will hear me shout

New love, I surrender to myself

My last deep breath I looked into myself

This new life I have chosen

The old life has been frozen

Rico, don't look back

Free your mind and the rest will follow

Understand the new you

Look up, the sun is shining on you

This new movement just makes me listen-learn-smile

Have an open heart that can heal itself when pain arrives

The hearts are fun to have

The shining sun has been good on my behalf

The new love I truly have for myself

I found my new family and friends at Free Minds

And I wish to have a greater success with you guys

B-4 I Write

by Myron

B-4 I write / my brain ignites / that's RIGHT

And just like Mike / my thoughts take FLIGHT

Into another dimension / that's far beyond EARTH

That's what occurs / then my brain starts to give BIRTH

It goes up outta here into a whole new STRATOSPHERE

Where there's no fear / thoughts come clear beyond my YEARS

And there's a certain feeling that comes over ME

That inspires me to write down REALITY

Then I analyze, then I CATEGORIZE

Circumstances and situations through my EYES

That I must confess / I write truth nothing LESS

And that's 4 real / because I been blessed / by the BEST

To me it seems like / there's nothing more REAL

Than to rhyme articulately 'bout how I FEEL

It makes me feel fine / to write between the LINES

'Cause it makes people see the power of my MIND

To me / writing will be a never-ending SEQUEL

'Cause it's mind stimulating and plus I teach PEOPLE

In a precise way / of ABSTRACT ART

'Cause it forms in my mind / but releases from my HEART

And because of that / there's no way to stop IT

Writing in rhyme form on any given TOPIC

Like Steph Curry's jump shot / it's all in the WRIST

We do what we do easy, because it's our GIFT

Ready for a Change
by Harold

Estoy listo para un cambio en mi vida
Listo para un cambio de pensamientos
Listo para un cambio de actitud
Listo para un cambio en mis estudios
Listo para un cambio de amigos
Listo para un cambio en mi vocabulario
Listo para un cambio con mi comportamiento

I am ready for a change in my life
Ready for a change in my thoughts
Ready for a change in attitude
Ready for a change in my studies
Ready for a change of friends
Ready for a change in my vocabulary
Ready for a change in my behavior

Donald
(conversation)

I grew up in this community, two blocks from the school I now work for, and it was somehow communicated to us that it's a badge of honor to say, "I've been locked up." As crazy as it sounds. There's so many misrepresentations about being incarcerated: *Man, they gave you big pancakes, and they give you this and that. And you get to lift weights all day. And they have a football team down there.* People are fed a lot of those stories. They give you the impression they just went away to a resort or something. And once you start thinking like that, the deterrent that jail or prison is supposed to be, is no longer a deterrent to stopping crime. So, if I'm tempted to get in this stolen car, *Well, the worst that can happen is I go to jail. Maybe that's not so bad.*

I would say upwards of 65% of our students have someone in the family who either has been, or is currently, incarcerated. And most of the boys that come into this group[1] have somebody in the family incarcerated, in many cases their father. You know, that leaves a huge hole and it really impacts the growth and development of boys. I think it's caused a lot of the boys to have difficulty in relating to other men, to have issues when it comes to self-value, and to get disillusioned about life and what it has to offer. To think that this is kind of the way it has to be. You know: *This is the way it was for my dad, and so, more than likely, I'll probably get locked up, too.* As opposed to understanding that there's roads to avoid this.

---

1   The Lion Hearts Book Club, a group that Donald founded to support his young students

*Donald shares his perspective as a teacher and counselor in a
school and community where many of the students live with the
consequences of family members who are incarcerated.*

That you don't have to fall into this trap. That through education, through developing strong work habits, through being proactive about getting yourself in a position to earn income, you can avoid that.

So I said, I'm going to build something for young males to teach them how to be mentally strong. Because there weren't those people there for me. We wanted to start a young men's group. And the school mascot is a lion, so we decided to call it Lion Hearts Book Club. We used the book *The Untold Story of the Real Me* by Free Minds sort of as a guidebook to talk about incarceration. And the guys just kind of fell in love with the book; they could really identify with it: *Hey, that sounds like me. That sounds a lot like how I feel.* You know: *I've seen that myself. My uncle does that, or my older brother.* It becomes group therapy.

We share. We talk about how all these things are relevant to our manhood and maturity and so forth. Some of the issues that the authors talk about in the book—fatherlessness, poverty, drugs, witnessing crime on the street—are so relevant to our young people here at this school. They're faced with these challenges. And it's like Vegas in the room, you know, everything has to stay in here. The boys expect that from each other. They feel the brotherhood. It creates bonds. It gives them opportunity for a disclosure and brainstorming. And they give a lot of suggestions. *Well, maybe you could approach it like this. This is the way I handled it when I lost my father. Or when my father was shot. This is what I thought about it. This is what I tried not to think about.* So it becomes very peer-supportive and instructive.

And it's so valuable, having the Free Minds authors come and say, "Hey, you don't want to do what I've done. I know what I'm

talking about, and don't go this way." And because the authors attribute some of how they got incarcerated to being a boy who harbored these feelings and maybe didn't get the right supports, it has helped me highlight the importance of getting support for your feelings and emotions. Because, we see where this can lead to you making these bad choices. Letting your impulses and anger take over. Maybe picking up a gun, maybe going violently or aggressively at somebody. So, we talk about solutions. About how, if we don't plan *not* to go [to jail], that we can end up going. If we don't make a specific plan for our life and have a structured set of values we live by and objectives.

And I'm seeing kids start to make changes in behavior in the classroom. I've seen kids say that, *hey, I'm going to start taking better care of my body and make a commitment not to use drugs* and things like that. I think it's stimulated some of them to value their achievement more. It's stimulated some of them to invest in their creativity, and to write problems out. And that's a good way to cope and handle your angry feelings and your stressors.

I, myself, struggled in many areas coming up—and narrowly escaped. I mean, through the power of God because I was on a downward track. I was in and out of various legal troubles and even spending juvie time. I went to the high school right up the road, Ballou. And the assistant principal told my mother at that time that, if she has any other children, Miss Ross, put your investment in them. Because this one right here, he's going to be locked up or dead. But very shortly after that—I was 17—I got really wholeheartedly embraced at church. God helped to transform my life. I got connected with a young lady who became my girlfriend, and she was very scholastically inclined. She had applied at a lot of schools. And she slipped in

an application for me, too, which I never would have done.
I had something coming up in the courts. My co-defendant
got locked up for four years. But because she had applied
to a school for me—unbeknownst to me—I received an
acceptance from a Christian college in Alabama. The judge
was so impressed, and he said this is not a guy who we need
to incarcerate; he's trying to do something with himself. He
said, young man, this is your blessed day: the court is going to
give you a scholarship. You're going to go down to the school
in Alabama. It serves two purposes for us. It gets you off of
the street. It gives you an opportunity to go to school. He said,
but if you fail this court, if you bring back anything below a C,
this court is going to be asking for your grades. You're going to
be supervised by Madison County probation and supervision
while you're down there. So, I went to college. With my
girlfriend, who became my wife. And I sent back the grades.
And everything went well. God is good. God is good.

When I came back, I went to see that assistant principal. At the
time, I never knew what he said. My mom hid that from me
because she didn't want to break my spirit. He remembered
me, and he was just blown away at this person that I was. He
said, you can really be instructive and helpful to a lot of these
young men. I'm going to hire you. So, I come home and tell
my mom that I'm hired by this guy. *You're hired by that guy? Do
you know what he said about you?* I never spoke to him about
what he said, but he hired me. He told a lot of students about
transformations I made—and a light bulb went off for him, he
got it. So that's how I got into the school system 30 years ago.
I was 21 years old.

It is a great reminder never to write anybody off. Never to
count anybody out. And that's what happens so much to

people in the criminal justice system. We write them off once they go in there, count 'em out. Where some of these guys who come out and get involved in the Free Minds program, they're going to do things that are going to blow some people's minds. I'm so impressed with the people that come here and their ability to articulate and express themselves, that I can see them doing great things in the community. If someone would give them a chance.

When I Write

by Asante

When I write, I express my mind
It also helps me skip through time
I go through too much
I don't know what to do
I lost both parents
Now I'm left lost with no clue
I'm on my own
I'm no longer a child
Sometimes I be overwhelmed
I feel like a big cow
Having thoughts of giving up
It's too much pain
Picturing my son
All I see is what's left to gain
God knows I got a lot to lose
That's why I feel
I have something to prove

Resilient

by Antoine

Resilient is a strong word like *education*

A young man from Southeast

That's resilient in the making

Don't judge me on my past or my future situation

Judge me on my character

And not the hard times that I'm facing

I'm strong

I'm wise

I'm independent

I'm smart

My future is bright

My past looks dark

I read

I write

Go to class and succeed

My body is incarcerated

But my mind is totally freed!

I Forgive Me
by Mark

Can't keep thinking of my past
I need to forgive myself
I need to move forward
I'm giving up the darkness
I want the sun
So finally...
I forgive me

FOR THE
TIME LOST

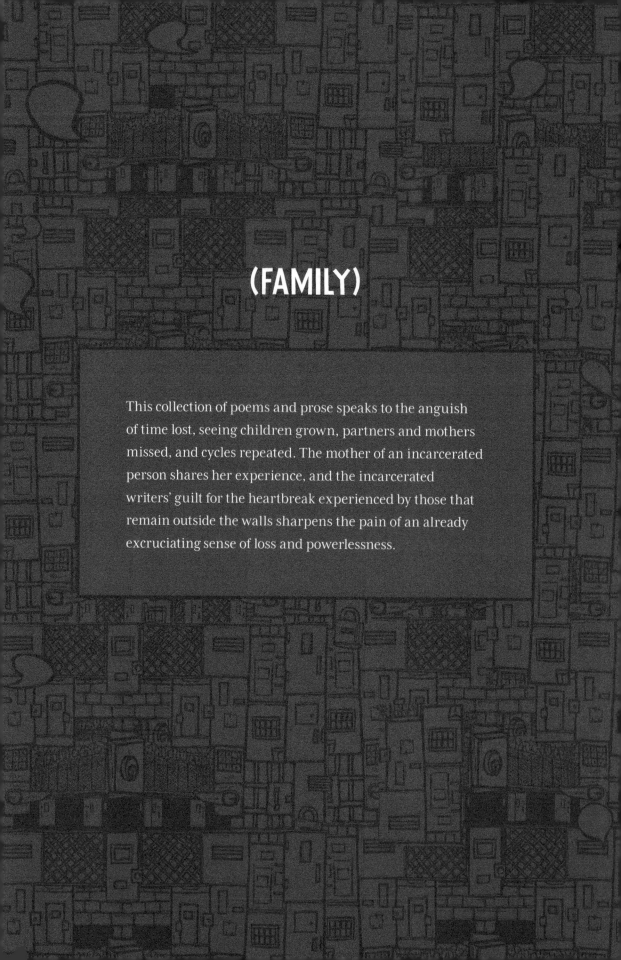

(FAMILY)

This collection of poems and prose speaks to the anguish of time lost, seeing children grown, partners and mothers missed, and cycles repeated. The mother of an incarcerated person shares her experience, and the incarcerated writers' guilt for the heartbreak experienced by those that remain outside the walls sharpens the pain of an already excruciating sense of loss and powerlessness.

A poem from a father to his youngest son

by Timothy

The worst pain I've ever felt
was looking at you, reach for me
through a video screen and I couldn't
touch you; right then, I knew
what it felt like to die, a living death

A Father's Thought

by Travis

Bad world, good girl, teeth as white as pearls

Eyes as gray as the skies on a rainy day

Long dark hair

Her perfume is a candy scent that pollutes the air

Her essence reeks of perfection

Made from God's mold

Thoughts as clean as Jesus' soul

She brings peace to a mad mind

Infuses happiness to the sad times

Makes good of the bad vibes

Her smile glistens

I heard rhymes as she strides

Rooted to rise

As a tree by the water's side

She stands strong

Words as sweet as an angel's song

For years, I've loved the thought of you

Your mother brought me you

Thanks to my higher power

In my final hour

My every minute spent with you

I'll be glad and I'll thank God I'm your dad

To my daughter, Aaliyah

Can't wait to see you,

Your father

My Little Flower

by Antwon

Sometimes silence is the loudest of noises
And her silence speaks volumes
Everybody is entitled to make mistakes and in
Life we all stumble
But of all the mistakes I could have made
With this one I scarred her for life
To leave her alone to raise our child
Was like condemning her to a rough life
We may not have been the best of lovers
But for 9 months, she carried our daughter
So strong she appears on the surface
On the inside she feels dirty, used
And worthless
And no matter where she turns, she is
Overwhelmed with pain
So she runs back to the game
Like a moth to a flame
Run, child, run
You're still my little flower

I can only imagine how much resentment
My daughter holds for me
And believe me it's there if she's anything
Like me
I once hated even the thought of my father
There were so many bottled up
Emotions towards him I harbored
Now as a man I see how he felt
To have to wonder as a father if his

Child's being raised by someone else
To be stripped of a chance to love
His only child
To be separated by so many miles
Man, I may not have been what they
Call a "model citizen"
But I'm still a man that loves and
Misses his children
And the last thing I will ever be is a
Coward
Kool, I pray God helps you bloom into
The most beautiful little flower

Deboria
(conversation)

My mother really wasn't there as I grew up. So I became grown
and had my first child at a *very* young age. I didn't know that
my mother had a mental illness. Back in them days, if you said
you have a mental illness, you got locked down. But it caused
issues. So I was trying to take care of my daughter, and then
I turned around and had Pete. That's when *my* mental illness
kicked in. Because it was the suffering of a young child having
young babies. Their father, he was an abuser. So I had to leave
him once my son was two. And my daughter was four.

I raised my kids to the best of my ability. I worked and
everything. But then, as my kids got a little older, I got
involved in drugs. And my kids got away from me. Pete might
have been maybe like 10 or something when he was getting
into stuff. I tried to keep him under my wings, but I got caught
up in my own stuff. My daughter, she was, like, in the seventh
grade. And she would run away from home.

When I lost control of them, it really hurt. I lost hope. So I kept
doing [drugs]. I kept getting locked up because when you got
this disease, your disease makes you do things that you never
thought you would do. So I started shoplifting. And, in the
process of shoplifting, kept getting locked up. As I was getting
locked up, my kids was doing what they wanted to do.

So this one particular time, the judge said to me that I just
can't do this no more. I said, "Well, okay, Your Honor. Let me
go home and explain to my kids that I'm going to jail and I

won't be back for a little while." And that's what I did. I came
home, and I had a meeting with both of them. And I told
them that I would not be home, that I'll be gone for a while.
So please stay out of trouble. Pete was 16 and my daughter was
18. A month later, my daughter came to see me in jail. She
said, "Ma, Pete just went to jail for murder." It hurt my heart.
I just wanted to die. My son just went to jail for murder. My
daughter was graduating. I wasn't there for her graduation.
And there wasn't nothing I could do.

They charged him as an adult, they brought him over to jail. I
kept trying to tell them, "I need to see my son." But I couldn't.
And every day I prayed, *God, don't let something happen to my
son*. And I was really worried about my daughter being out
here by herself. Because both of us was over at the jail. My
visiting days was Mondays and Thursdays. His visiting days
was Tuesdays and Fridays. Do you know, every visiting day
my daughter came to see her mother and her brother?
Every visiting day.

When I went to the feds, he was going through court. So they
called me, and the lady from Pretrial Services,[1] she said, "You
was a disgraced mother that you allow your son to catch a
murder charge. Your son's getting 25 years." I mean, if I could
have got through the phone, I probably would be locked up
right with him with a murder charge. But there wasn't really
too much I could say because I was in my case manager's office
when this lady called and was telling me all this.

---

1   Pretrial Services Agency refers to the agency that supervises defendants
     released to the community and makes recommendations to the court.

*Deboria shares her perspective as a mother whose son
was incarcerated and who was incarcerated herself.*

Once I came home, my son was down at Lorton,[2] behind the big wall. That was maximum security. So, 16 years old, he's locked down 23 hours. So that hurt me. I'm, like, *Oh, somebody's going to hurt my son. My son is going to get hurt.* And that all stayed on my mind. I couldn't stay clean. I was so worried. Because, like I say, I got a disease of addiction. If you want to know the truth, I was addicted to anything that changed my mood. From pills, cough syrup, heroin, cocaine. Anything that changed my mind. But my *main* thing was heroin. And, along with my disease of addiction, I have a mental illness that's called depression. I work in the field now. Because when you got that type of experience, you know, you need to give it back much as you can. I deal with the mentally ill, substance abuse, domestic violence.

Now, I didn't know that that's what I had until I went into recovery and talked to a psychiatrist. That was after the incarceration and everything. He told me that was my diagnosis. February the 2nd, 1997, I went into a treatment center. And I have not looked back since. I have 24 years clean. And that came from listening to other people that have been through what I've been through and knowing that I got to do this for my son—to help my son. Because if we're going to lay down and suffer, we're going to get depressed and we're going to kill our own self. And they still going to be in there. They're going to worry about you. So you can't do that.

Wherever my son was at, believe me, we went. I would go see him or I'd send some money if I couldn't go see him. When he left Lorton, he went to Ohio. Left Ohio. He was in Big Sandy, Kentucky. He went to Lewisburg, Pennsylvania. Yeah,

---

2 Lorton Reformatory served as the District of Columbia's prison until it closed in 2001.

he went some places. Everywhere they went always had bus trips. Some of the other ones that was far out, he said don't come. Because he knew that I would have jumped on a plane quick and went. I was trying to see my son every time it was available. And my daughter and her kids or somebody would go with me.

My biggest worries was the gangs in jail. I was hoping and praying that I didn't have to have my son come home in a box. Because I had a friend and the day he was getting out [of jail], he got in a fight, and the guy stabbed him in the heart. So I know how the deaths are in there. All I was thinking about was how I was going to get him out of there.

It's like I was still locked up too. Because I had to pray for my child. I had to worry about my child.

Like, when the guards beat my son and locked my son down, and somebody had called me and told me what happened, and I called down there. So I said, "Since y'all want to do that. I'm going to call Eleanor Holmes Norton's[3] office. I'm going to call Channel 7. I'm sending *everybody* down there." Next thing I know, they shipped my son out and put him in a two-year program. And my son been going through that program. My son has so many certificates that the stuff he done did—he done got his GED, he just did everything.

I always tell my son, God has the key, and God has the answer. For you still in there, it's a plan that God has. You know, because he could have let you out at any time, but he don't

---

3   Eleanor Holmes Norton is the District of Columbia's Delegate to the U.S. House of Representatives. As the Delegate, she is entitled to vote in committee but cannot participate in legislative floor votes because DC is not a state.

want you out here. See, because a lot of my son's friends got killed. And he would have been out here. He might have got killed. But he's out here now, and he's amazing. He got out December 11th, 2020. And the director of the jail—everybody did not want him to leave. You know, all you could hear was good things about Pete from officers and everybody. He was the mentor for some young boys that's getting ready to go to the federal system.

When he got home, he didn't want a lot of people. No, no, no, no, no, no, no, no, no, no. Uh-uh. He said, "Ma, I don't need to be around a whole lot of people." Because everybody was trying to take him out that first night. He say, no, I go to Subway then I can go home and go to sleep. I think he just wanted to have some peace at home. You know, get adjusted to society. Because not only has it changed for him, it's like the whole world is changing. But my son is adapting. He has adapted. It's amazing.

I'm most proud of my son that he went to jail and did all them years and came out to be the man he's supposed to be. I know he had dreams and all of that. But, like I told him: that was then. Your youth dreams are gone, but your adult dreams— your goals, and everything—all that can come true.

My Baby

by Joseph

At infancy taken to the grandparents' home
Grandma holding me gently while shaping the dome
Momma softly scratching cradle cap with the tip of a comb
Both of them grooming their baby

Toddler years taking high, awkward steps
Uncles are youngsters playing pranks on the newest whelp
Sometimes I'd smile and laugh but other times I'd yelp
Grandma yelling, "Ya'll stop teasing my baby!"

Age eleven, tears pour out the eyes
Questioning how God could let my grandmomma die
Momma reading from a Bible while trying to explain why
Trying her best to comfort her baby

High school ball-star, blocks and dunks
Girls in tight skirts showing off their rump
All tryna holla, but none of them I want
But then see her and I'm thinking, "D*mn, baby"

Time to make our love official, about to be a father
Patiently awaiting the child's gender from the family doctor
One last pushhh, the wife gives birth to a daughter
Crying tears of joy—look at our baby

One daughter, two daughters, three daughters
Oh!
Love is a beautiful thing, but can be a burden to hold
Bills and expenses direct stress to our souls

Wife looks to me so I mumble, "D*mn, baby"

Crime doesn't pay and crime never will
But it temporarily took care of the bills
Had to make some people shriek and make others shrill
Justifying crime to feed our babies

Lights out! Staring at the darkness in a cell
No more wife, no freedom, just a mind filled with hell
Momma brings two kids to visit so I'll know all is well
On one knee, I'm hugging my babies

10 years, 20 years, the daughters are grown
Missed all their childhoods because I couldn't be home
The youngest daughter now has a child of her own
"She looks just like my grandmother!"
My baby

Mother

by Keven

I hate to think about the day
when I will have to say good-bye,
yet there are times when I believe
that maybe I should just try.

I keep holding on to each day,
praying that things will get better.
Like constantly awaiting mail call,
in hopes of receiving just one little letter.

Loss is never an easy thing to face
regardless of the events that follow,
but loss caused by my own actions
is a much harder pill to swallow.

They say there's no stronger love
than that of a mother's own.
If this is really the truth,
then why am I so alone?

There are truly no words
that express how I feel.
The pervasive loneliness throughout my soul
is like a cold, hard piece of steel.

I've been trying to move on with my life,
but I just can't seem to let go.
Because that would mean I accept a truth:
a truth I just don't want to know.

I've been told by many people
to grieve for you as if you're gone,
but it would be just a big façade
besides the fact, I'd know it'd be wrong.

I'd rather believe that you'll come around
and I'll continue to find ways to cope,
than believe you've given up on me
and I've chosen to give up all hope.

Though I haven't always shown it,
I've always loved you with all my heart.
I pray each night to God above
that we can find a way to a new start.

I can't undo the things I've said or done:
whether they've been good, bad, small, or great.
I'm just asking for us to move on
before we wait and wait until it's too late.

So please, hear my crying words
as I am asking for forgiveness.
Because not another day I want to go by
where it is my mother that I have to miss.

Rafael
(conversation)

I was named for my father. They called me Rafael, after him.
My father was 16 when he got locked up. He's 40-something
now. He's serving a life sentence. And yeah, I ended up
becoming a Title 16[1] kid, just like him.

When I was growing up, my mom worked hard. She was a
police officer. You don't tell nobody that in the streets. But as a
kid, I wanted to be a police officer just like her. One day, when
I was about 10, I told my father this on the phone. He was like,
Nah, you don't want to be police! They the ones put me in here! So,
after that, I never wanted to be a police officer anymore. I
wanted nothing to do with them.

My mom used to take me to see him at the DC Jail. I remember
trying to see him through that dirty, scratched up glass with
trash and nastiness everywhere. When he got to federal
prison, we'd drive all day long just to see him. I used to get
nervous butterflies in my stomach as we got closer. I don't
really know why. I guess it was because I wanted so much for
him to think highly of me. During one visit he asked me how
many push-ups I could do. I got down on the floor and did
some and he was happy. I wanted to impress him so I kept
going and even did the ones where you push off the ground
and clap your hands before you land. He was *real* happy about
that, which made me feel so good. I never got to be around my
dad other than that—like spend a day together from sun up to

---

1   Title 16 refers to the DC code that states that juveniles can be charged
     as adults.

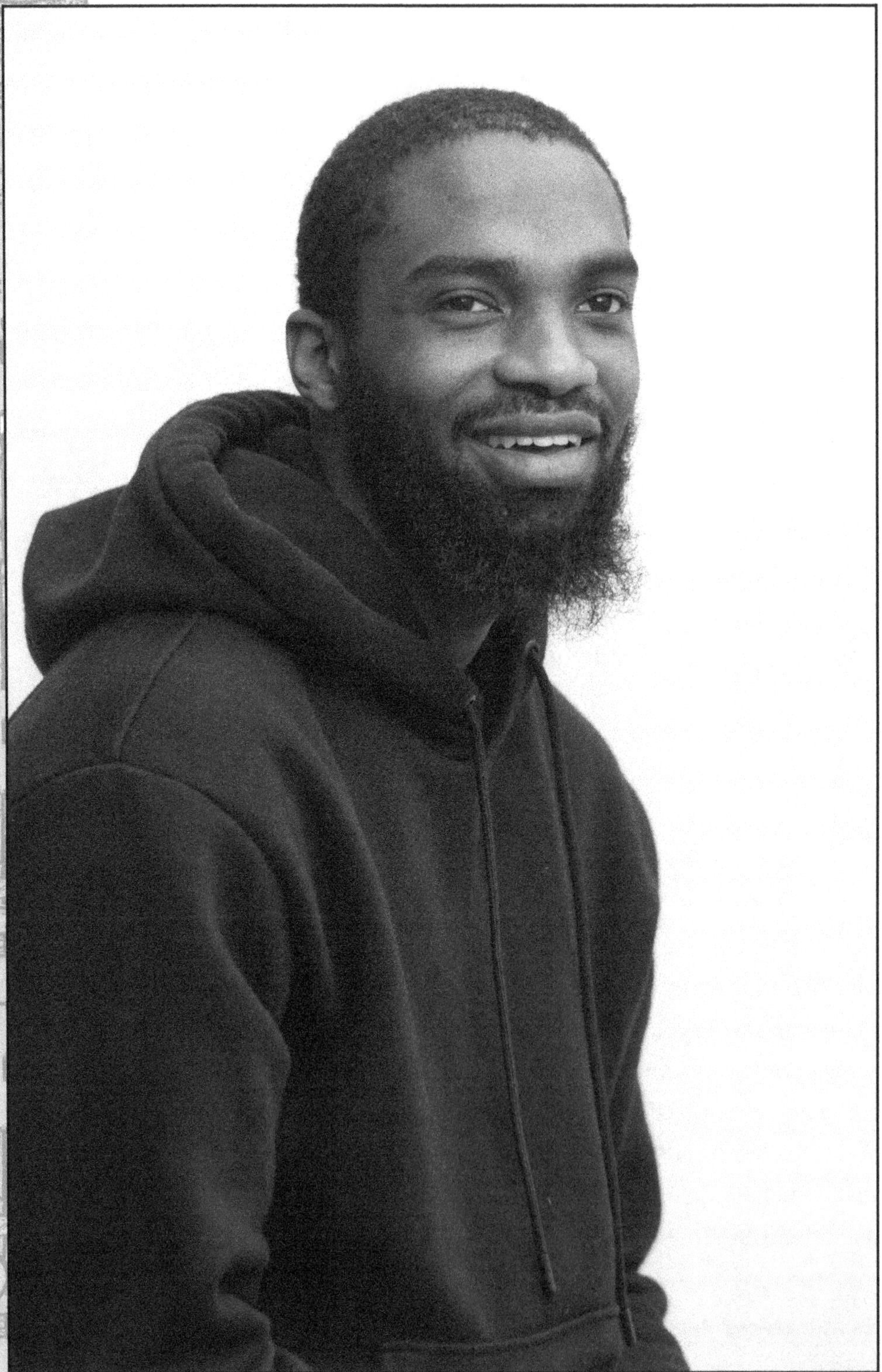

sun down. He's been in jail my whole life.

I used to hear everyone in my neighborhood talk about how my father ran wild in the streets. His mother—my grandmother—was using drugs and I think he had it difficult. But I was always hearing how tough he was. They'd call me "Little Raf." It made me happy, and even though I didn't really know him, it made me aspire to be just like him.

It didn't take long. I was always good in school, and I thought I'd go to college one day, but at the same time, the streets was tugging at me. I think my father's incarceration definitely had an effect on me. I had so many family members in the street. The older dudes, they would encourage us to steal bikes and stuff. I just wanted to be a part of it all. All human beings want to fit in. So I started running the streets in middle school.

I was 16 when I was arrested and charged as an adult. I was being a follower. My young mind just wasn't even developed. I knew right from wrong, but I was being an idiot. I wish I hadn't been there. And I wish it hadn't happened. I think about it all the time and I feel sad.

Going to jail at that age was surreal and traumatizing. Being around grown men who got nothing on their minds beyond getting high or beefing. I didn't feel like I could relate to anyone. I did time in solitary. I was locked in my cell for an entire year. Overall, I just felt lost, disconnected, and hopeless.

I was still at the DC Jail waiting to be sentenced when I was 18. I was on the phone with my grandmother when she told me my father had been sent back to the jail and was on the same unit that I was. At that time, they kept the two tiers of the unit

separate. I worked detail on the midnight shift though and the CO^2 liked me. That night, she took me over and opened my father's cell. We hugged. We just couldn't stop laughing when we saw each other.

As it turned out, my two uncles and a cousin ended up on the same unit. My father hadn't seen my uncle since he was a baby! Most people have family reunions at a picnic in a park. We had ours in the DC Jail. We were ecstatic. We really enjoyed it. I even got to share a cell with my father. He was like, *This is the bomb!* He used words like that sometimes. We had a good year together. We got real close. He's a good man with a big heart. But eventually, he had to go. When he departed, it was sad, but we didn't get teary-eyed. I was just happy for the time we had.

I know my father never wanted a life like this for me. I don't know exactly what it is he wished for me, but in jail or in the streets was not it. I work hard to keep my focus on the future. I got my high school diploma, and then enrolled in college in prison. I graduated with an associate degree in business. I have big plans for my life. I hope I'll have a child one day. People talk about the cycle of incarceration. And all those years ago, visiting my dad in prison, I never thought I'd be behind bars too. But my child will never get locked up. My child will never be in the type of environment that will lead them to jail or prison. I know how important that is. I know this for sure. This cycle ends with me.

---

2   Correctional Officer

Rafael served nearly 11 years in prison starting at the age of 16 before being granted compassionate release due to health complications during the COVID-19 pandemic. He is enjoying time with his family, studying the stock market, and working for his mother's event planning company. He plans to continue his college studies to obtain a bachelor's degree in business information technology.

Family

by Craig

I shed a tear for the time lost
My heart crossed over the years
The memories I've come across
I cherish as priceless as a family
We've endured every crisis
Laughed, cried, gave birth and buried
Learned about what life is to the point
I see the light with closed eyelids
Fatherless family look to mothers for everything
She did her best to make her son a man
I often wonder how my mom did it
Understand the furthest thing from my mind
Was neglecting my family tree.
It's part of my every vein.

Missing Momma

by Daniel K.

I've had no visits in five long years,

what makes it worse, my family isn't near.

I reflect on all the good times as a child at home,

but after a decade, those memories have faded; almost gone.

I still remember my Momma's smell, sound, and infectious smile,

it leaves me yearning to go back in time to be a child.

Oh how I'd change a lot of the things that I did,

maybe I could have escaped this 25 year bid.

I should have listened to all my Momma had said,

I pray I make it out of prison before she's dead.

No violence, no inmate, no officer scares me as bad,

as I am of losing her; d*mn I'd be so sad.

So I must push forward and show her a new man,

hopefully she hangs on long enough, I believe she can.

So Momma, you're the only woman in my life, and I'm your son,

and just as I end each letter and phone call...I love you more than infinity
    plus one!

A Letter to Myself

by Samuel

Dear Sam,

Get it right
Time is ticking away quickly
Stage IV
5 cm. x 7 cm.[1]

Get it right
Spend as much time with her as possible
Don't explode
Make allowances

Get it right
Get out of here ASAP
Kick the habit
Don't come back

Get it right
Make the time count
Love her like never before
Hold on tight

Get it right!

As always,
Sam

---

1   This poem refers to the poet's mother's cancer diagnosis and the size of the tumor.

Hello Son

by Ronny

Dear Son
My baby boy
My eldest
My first-born joy

I carried you
Counted your fingers and toes
Prayed for your heart
I watched you grow

I scolded you
When you went wrong
I dried your tears
I sang you a song

Days gone by
Now you're a man
A wife and kids
A career, a plan

You broke my heart
When you went away
Where's the man I raised
My baby boy?

You came to me
On your broken knees
"Mama, I'm so sorry
Take me home, please"

You must have forgot
I brought you to life
I'd do anything for you
I'd face any strife

I know you're afraid
You've got all those years
I hate what you've done
I've cried my own tears

Remember my son
There's nothing to fear
You're always my baby
I'll always be here

You may not get it
But thank God above
Nothing compares
To your mother's love

LIFE AFTER INCARCERATION

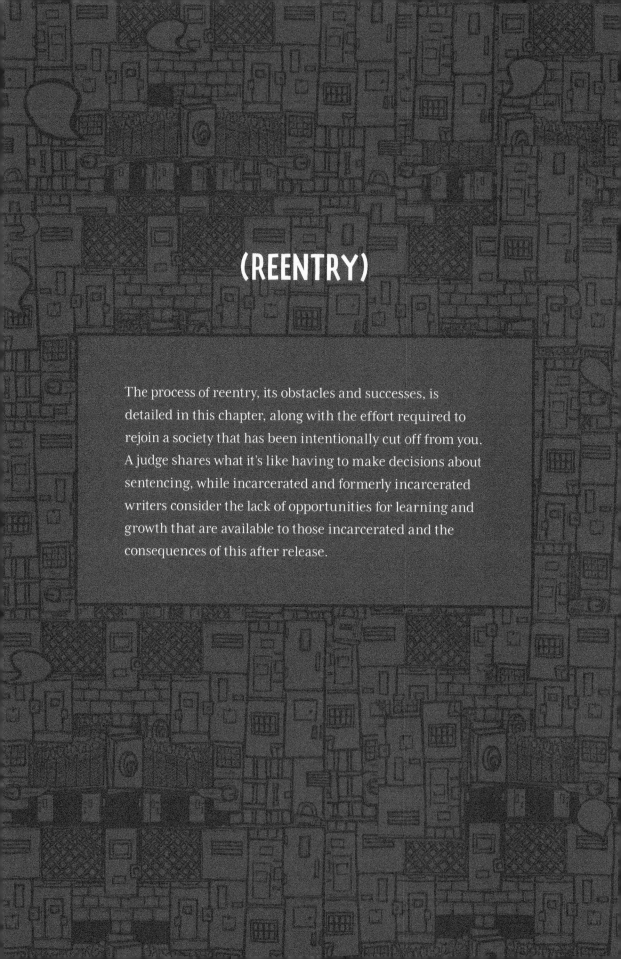

(REENTRY)

The process of reentry, its obstacles and successes, is detailed in this chapter, along with the effort required to rejoin a society that has been intentionally cut off from you. A judge shares what it's like having to make decisions about sentencing, while incarcerated and formerly incarcerated writers consider the lack of opportunities for learning and growth that are available to those incarcerated and the consequences of this after release.

Todd
(conversation)

It's never easy to sign the order sending someone to prison,
even if you firmly believe they deserve it. It's my least favorite
part of the job, and I think most of my colleagues' least favorite
part of the job. But I think you're playing a role in protecting
the community. And it can be great and meaningful and
terrible and depressing, all at once.

The hardest ones are the young people. The most frequent
crime appears to be, mostly these days, robberies. Street
robberies. Mostly unarmed. For some of the kids, that's going
to be the worst thing they ever do. And for some, they're on the
way to doing other things. And they're at such fragile points.
One of the things I know from being at PDS[1] is how bad prison
can be for someone that age, and how it can really change
the trajectory of their life. We hear a lot about people who are
scared straight in prison. But that, I don't think, is really the
norm and expectation. I've found, usually people came out of
prison more likely to be dangerous than before they went in.

[While a public defender] I had one kid who's somebody I
think about a lot. Because he was a really sweet kid. He was
the oldest of six or seven in his family. Single mom. There was
a fight in his housing complex and his mother went to break it
up and got hit by one of the participants in the fight with some
kind of object. He then went back to his house and came out
with, like, a one-shot rifle, 0.22. And, depending on who you
believe, was protecting his mother, and shot the kid. Didn't kill

---

1   PDS refers to the DC Public Defender Service.

Todd shares his perspective as a judge and former public defender.

him. It's amazing, from the distance he was, that he actually hit him. We lost the trial. And he got a 10-year sentence. But his conviction was reversed on appeal. And so he came back from the federal prisons in four years.

I met him at the jail before the hearing. He had changed. He was a different guy. He wasn't the same kid anymore. He was so much more pent-up, so much more sophisticated—and estranged a little bit from his family. Then, maybe less than five years after that, he was arrested and convicted for one of the most brutal murders you'd ever heard of. You can't really turn back time, but I really do think that his time in prison was instrumental in that happening. I really don't think he was that kind of person before who would have done that.

As a judge, those are the cases that really keep you up at night in terms of, What do you do? You know, this kid who is at that crossroads. A lot of them have been ripped off by the school system. Had really hard family lives. Had been maybe through the juvenile system or even the child neglect system and not gotten that much out of it. A lot of them have sort of mixed records. They're kind of involved in school enough that you're thinking, do I take them out of this, or not? And so there's that incredible tension of, If I decide this is the kind of case where the kid should do some time in adult prison, is he going down the path of my client? Or, if I decide to try to keep him in the community—we've all had situations in which we've made that choice and the person wound up doing something else violent. The first thing they look at is the judge who released them. And so there's a very natural tendency to think that the judge is, you know, "safer" by locking them up. And if you decide to give somebody a very punitive sentence, you're never criticized. The press never says, *This judge locked this person up,*

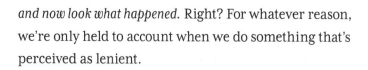

and now look what happened. Right? For whatever reason, we're only held to account when we do something that's perceived as lenient.

And, at the same time, the people you give a chance to—you put on probation, you give programs—you're very likely to not see them again. They're out of sight, out of mind. And so, when you're on a calendar where you're doing a lot of probations, you get this steady trickle of violation reports, and it feels like everyone is violating. And that's not the case. But it gets into your mind that it's not working because you just never hear from the people who it *does* work for.

You forget about them because you just don't see them again. And so, again, you have to guard against the impression that this never works.

I think that is an opportunity for advocates to change the conversation by letting people know that *not* incarcerating people has benefits. That's what we need to hear more about. That there are all these people where the judge made a decision to keep them in the community, and they took advantage of it and proved that to be the right decision.

Dedicated Patience

by Shannon

Dedicated patience,
a journey of frustration with the adaptation
of returning back to a society
that lacks the proper preparation
that leads to minimum employment opportunities
with insufficient wages.

Dedicated patience
is life after incarceration
the struggle of a nation
of sons of the forgotten fathers
of 40 acres lost from past sins in a field of destruction,
inequality and too much hatred.

Dedicated patience
where excellence and greatness is prevalent
yet the struggle of BLM exemplifies
everyday failure of relations and not just communication
but lost opportunities for progress
and financial elevation,
a direct result of misrepresentation and centuries of miseducation.

Dedicated patience
is what it takes to succeed when you are expected to fail
but free my brother and watch in wonder
as he rise and continue to prevail
win after win driven by a strong will
as we prove all wrong yet again.

Hope

by Aneka

I hope I grow up one day
I hope I live to see 90+
I hope the anger in me goes away
I hope I don't just give up
I hope I'll have a family soon
I hope someone claims me as their own
I hope I'll still see the sun and moon
Each day is a blessing and I won't give up
I hope I can right my wrongs
I hope I can start over new
I want to be a better person
And not a simple fool
I hope prison changes me for the better
I don't want to be institutionalized
I hope this keeps me from stealing
And telling stupid lies
Now I'm free!
I can finally make things right
No more hoping
It's time to live my life

The Old Me/The New Me

by Hure

The Old Me

The old me would not care

The old me would not share

The old me would lie, steal

And cheat to feed my family

The old me would say, "I'm a man"

But live like a boy

The old me would say, "I'm strong..."

When I really felt weak

The old me would say, "I don't need anyone"

The old me would hang and gang bang

With no care who got hurt

While I did my dirt

The old me would always make my mother cry

The old me would want to die

The old me never wanted to look in the mirror

But when the old me died

The new me showed me life more clear

The New Me

The new me smiles and is very thankful

The new me is honest and open

The new me makes my mother smile

The new me is not a cheater

The new me cares for the youth and all people

The new me wants to help the youth and teach the truth!

The new me is not afraid to be a man

And take a stand for the poor or the voiceless
The new me is not afraid to be educated
And fearless in my goals and in my dreams

Reentry

by Warren

Transitioning into a challenge

I wonder if my caliber of man

is significant enough to endure life ups and downs and unemployment
offices...

My family say they'll be there for me?!

True or False...

I guess we'll wait and see

Anxiety consumes me...

At ready, set, go where??

Because I don't have a home

I can call my own.

As I reflect on these smoke and mirrors,

"I'm ALONE!"

Hope and perseverance are my friends

These dudes provide the tools

I can use to unscrew the lid on OPPORTUNITY!

As I rise, I aspire to have all life's fruits

My first child, my first wife, a responsible life

21 years of incarceration

felt like a century,

in anticipation for a successful reentry

However, only fate knows what lies ahead for me

Today

by Donald

I woke up today and chose to lay

I chose to love

Made a conscious effort to thrive today

I opened doors today, in multiple ways

But some just to walk through

It was humbling

Walking without metal, I must get used to

Chuckling as I'm stumbling

I hugged a woman today

She shares the same blood as I

I didn't cry either

I smiled

To hug her again, I knew, wouldn't be a while

I ate eggplant parmesan today

It wanted pepper

But the option made it faster, better

I looked afar today

My vision—no limit

Today was cold

I chose to wear no jacket

Freedom kept me warm

Craig
(conversation)

I was released from prison in 2019 after serving 22 years and three months. I'd been behind bars since I was 17 years old. I knew I would go home one day. But actually walking out that door? It was crazy. My lawyer was there to meet me along with my sister. He was like, "You're free!" I was like, "Man, just get me in one of y'all cars!" I just wanted to put as much distance as I could between me and the jail. I didn't want to wait around and find out it was a mistake!

You spend years dreaming of being free and then you're finally released. People act like your troubles are over. But the hard part definitely ain't over. When you're in prison, all of your decisions are made for you. They tell you what cell to go to. They tell you what you're going to wear. They tell you your bed number. When you're released, that's when you find out you've never known a thing about the responsibilities of being an adult. You find out that the skills you learned in prison don't serve you at all in the outside world.

I felt like I didn't know how to do anything. I needed to get my ID. Without it you can't cash a check, get a job, nothing. I went to the DMV by myself. I sat there all day waiting for my number to get called. When it was finally my turn, the lady was like, "Man, we can't help you. You don't have the right papers." There were so many people around and I ain't understand what was going on. I told her, "I just came out of prison. I never experienced this." She just said, "I can't help you." And everybody just stood there looking at me. I felt so

embarrassed. Like I was different from everybody else who knew what to do.

I didn't even know how to ride the train. I went to meet up with my buddy. I asked the security guard, "How do you put money on this card?" and he showed me. I saw other people hitting the thing, going through with their card. So, I just copied what they doing. Once I got downstairs though, it got real. I just stood there watching all these trains come and go, and not knowing what to do. My buddy called and was, like, "Where you at?" I was, like, "Man, I don't know which way to go!" He told me to take the train to L'Enfant Plaza. When I got there, there were trains going everywhere! Downstairs, upstairs, hundreds of people. Everybody was moving and knew where they was going. They knew how to get out this door, how to get down those steps, how to move. I didn't know nothing. I called my buddy's phone, like, three times but he didn't answer. I didn't know what to do. I panicked. I was afraid to ask anyone for help. My buddy finally found me, and when I got with him, I felt safe. But before that, it was crazy. I stopped riding the subway for a long time after that.

Coming home taught me how much I was going to have to rely on other people to help me. One day I was up at the Free Minds office and I didn't have any way home. Another brother was going on the subway. He explained the subway map to me and showed me I could never really got lost. He stayed with me. I wrote down what he showed me and carried it in my pocket for a long time. Now I feel more comfortable and can ride the train again!

There are a lot of things other people know how to do, that I don't. Things I would have had a chance to learn if I'd grown

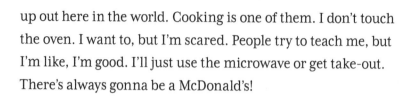

up out here in the world. Cooking is one of them. I don't touch the oven. I want to, but I'm scared. People try to teach me, but I'm like, I'm good. I'll just use the microwave or get take-out. There's always gonna be a McDonald's!

I was lucky. I got a job within a few weeks. But my supervisor was disrespectful to me. I wasn't trained on how to deal with conflict on the job. I called him on it and he ended up letting me go after just three months. In prison, we had all these job training programs and mock interviews, but they didn't really mean anything out here. Even some of the certifications I worked for in prison seemed useless. After I got fired, I spent five months straight applying for jobs. But I didn't even know how to fill out an application. I would get interviews and I got so nervous. Probably five different times I was told I had the job. But then something came up in my background check. I don't think people understand how hard it is. People think you have a fresh start. But you never really outrun a criminal record.

I remember I got a cleaning position up in some condos in Northwest DC. I'd be mopping the hallways and I'd notice some people kept their doors open or unlocked. I'd get so anxious that something would get misplaced or go missing. I just knew I would be one of the first suspects. I don't want to be anywhere if something bad might happen. If I am someplace and I find out drugs or anything else like that is going on, I won't stay around.

For the most part, I still feel most comfortable around other people that been in prison, or that work with an organization dealing with people that just came home. Being Black, there's already plenty of stigma against me. It's already in people's minds that a Black person is aggressive. That a Black person is always in the wrong. But being Black *and* an ex-offender with a felony? It feels like I always have such a long way to go just to prove myself.

Prison leaves marks on you. What I mean is it affected me emotionally. I come in the house and I still go straight to my room and shut my door. I only like to eat by myself in my room. I live with my sister and I know it bothers her sometimes. She and her friend will be eating at the table. But I don't join them. Now she leaves me a plate in the microwave. I'll heat it up and go to my room.

It affects my relationships. For example, not all women can deal with someone that just came off prison. I was only 17 when I went in, so the relationships I've had were different. Back then if you had a girlfriend, you just saw them when you saw them. But now women expect me to spend time with them and communicate. I'm not used to that. Sometimes I be in the house for hours just looking at the TV, or listening to the radio. I like to be by myself. In prison, when everyone went out for rec, it might be a beautiful day, but I used that time to be alone in my cell. I just wanted to enjoy the quiet. My family never dealt with nobody coming home from prison. A lot of times, they just don't know what to do.

People have always asked me about my goals. To be honest, I ain't really never had goals. In prison, it's different. Goals are more like, *I'm going to lose weight.* Or, *I'm going to start working out more.* And even though I knew I was going to get out of prison one day, when it actually happened I wasn't ready for the rest of my life. I ain't never really experienced nothing to know what I wanted. I just wanted to have a normal life to be honest.

Have a decent job and pay my bills.

Since I got out though, I think I've learned that helping other people is my calling. Even though I like to stay to myself, it makes me feel so good to help a person. For example, I was at a little clothing store a while ago and the lady in front of me didn't speak no English. She didn't have enough money and the guy was telling her she had to put something back. They weren't understanding each other and the guy was getting irritated with her. So I just asked him, "How much more she need?" He told me, "Man, you can't help. She needs like $19 and change." I pulled out $20 and put it on the counter. They were both surprised. But that's how I am.

More and more, I'm feeling like that is what I'm here to do—help other people. I don't do it to get no blessings. I've been blessed way before I started blessing others. On paper, I had a life sentence. I was going to die in prison. Coming home has been hard. I have to learn new things every day. I didn't know how to do much of anything. But making it back out here and just being humble, it's a blessing. So now I just want to live a normal life and help other people.

Craig served 22 years in prison from the age of 17. After release, he became the Free Minds Congressman John Lewis Fellow, and now works full-time on staff, providing peer support for other formerly incarcerated Free Minds members and assisting them with successfully navigating reentry. He was an instrumental advocate for the passage of DC's Second Look Amendment Act, which offers reconsideration to individuals who were given extreme sentences as young adults. Craig plans to pursue a career as a youth mental health practitioner.

WRITING MY
WAY OUT

(RESISTANCE)

Writing is celebrated in this chapter as a tool of hope and
resistance. A former prosecutor speaks to the inhumanity
of the justice system, while incarcerated and formerly
incarcerated writers demonstrate their power to reclaim their
own narratives and personal agency. They call for change and
progress, foster unity, show pride, and create new legacies.

They Don't Want Us to Recite Our Poems

by Arzell

They don't want us to recite our poems, don't want the people to behold any signs or see any symbols, and they d*mn sure don't want us to know that the ancestors are with us. They don't want us to recite our poems.

They fear the foreign sounds of our secret language: Hope. They thought it long dead. They are afraid of the spread of our fever, how it creeps along the senses—our hearing and seeing, our awakening perception, our ability to sniff out what's false.

The willingness to feel our most painful wound, the taste of blood on our lips. They don't want us to recite our poems.

They are afraid of the promise of our spring, the way Mother Earth blushes green for us, hiding her gift in full view of both the strong and weak alike.

She has shown us fine stones in a babbling brook: love, faith, courage, tenacity, and understanding. They fear the inevitable fall of their rampaging giants.

They don't want us to recite our poems. They want us to die with our songs unsung. They want to bury our burnt-out husks, perfectly preserved shells, with sightless eyes of bitter black smoke and a mouthful of tightly clenched pearl-white teeth, trapping inside, for all eternity, the music that they desperately fear.

They don't want us to recite our poems.

A Message to the Community:
A Letter from Prison
by Reggie

I offer my condolences to the families who have lost loved ones
And became victims to the violence

I offer my apologies for having been derelict in my duty and responsibility
    as a man
In not being the guardian, educator, and leader my communities needed
In order to be vital and life-affirming

I want to inform you that it is my goal to counteract the insanity of the
    destructive mindset
And I do not embrace those who prey upon any people
But particularly, my people

I want my voice to be heard:
Let the violence, drug dealing, physical, and spiritual abuse of the
    communities stop

As a man, I want it to be known that I have come to value and recognize
That the children need and deserve a safe and secure environment in which
    to grow and develop,
Be educated, have access to equal opportunities to excel,
And become who the Creator intended them to be

I ask that everyone reading or hearing this looks at a child
Whether at home, school, at play, in church, or mosque, and consider
    these words:

I am the African child

The whole world awaits my coming, all the earth watches with interest
To see what I shall become
Civilization hangs in the balance; for what I am, the world of tomorrow will be

I am the African child

You have brought me into this, about which I know nothing
You hold in your hand my destiny
You determine whether I shall succeed or fail
Give me, I beg you, a world where I can walk tall and proud
Train me, as is your duty unto me
To love myself, and my people
And to build and maintain a great nation
It is I who proclaim

I am the African child

The whole world awaits my coming, I shall not delay it
For I too have a dream

Voice of the People

by Gary

Roses is red...

But so is love...

And so is blood...

The administration dragged me through the mud

He threw up his hands

Officer Friendly threw a barrage of slugs

"Black Lives Matter"

That's a chant, chanted by the enchanted

Who's at a severe disadvantage

To some the term "revolutionary" seems romantic

Until death becomes a factor

Tears always comes after the laughter

Cuffs digging into the flesh after we're captured

Now we're exposed to the wrath of so called "Gods"

Who treat us like dogs

Who we look upon as hogs

Pigs...killing kids with bullets and bids

Manipulated by manipulators

Initiators and dictators

Dictate us, and watch us become rebellious

Power is the people, so they fear us

When you hear me, you hear us

    PREACH!!!

And as I teach

I aim to reach

Beyond the barrier that left you asleep

Wolves amongst sheep

In a dog-eat-dog world that's federal

I'm not eatable

The school of the hard knocks molded me into an intellectual
The plan is to conquer us with decimals
Which will leave us divided; undecided, kneeling to tyrants; herded across
    the Atlantic by pirates
I'm just being honest people
Stay tuned-in for the sequel

Jamila shares her perspective as a former prosecutor.

Jamila
(conversation)

I'm from Detroit, born and raised, and I grew up working class. I was the first in my family to graduate college and the first to go to law school. It had been a goal for me for so long. I had this vague notion that I wanted to help people and that, at times of change in our country, you saw lawyers at the forefront—civil rights lawyers and others. As a new lawyer, I remember asking a mentor for advice about what to do. He suggested the U.S. Attorney's Office in Washington, DC, which at the time, I thought was strange. You know, just being from Detroit and being a Black woman and thinking: *A prosecutor?* I just thought of them as folks who send people to prison.

But I also remembered distinctly an experience I had shadowing a public defender once, and how the answer to all of the questions she fielded from her client was, "Well, we have to see what the prosecutor says." Everything—from information on the case, to what the plea offer was going to be, to when that was going to happen—was up to the prosecutor. It really struck me that the prosecutor seemed to be one of the most powerful agents within the system. After I had a chance to understand that there were things that prosecutors could do other than sending people to prison, options like diversion and problem-solving courts, I thought it was important that someone with my background, who looked like me, have some of that power.

I had already seen the horrible impacts of incarceration on family members. I had cousins who had been incarcerated. It

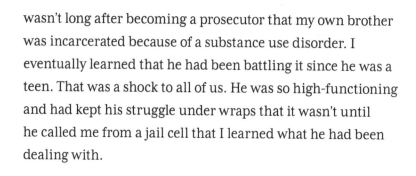

wasn't long after becoming a prosecutor that my own brother
was incarcerated because of a substance use disorder. I
eventually learned that he had been battling it since he was a
teen. That was a shock to all of us. He was so high-functioning
and had kept his struggle under wraps that it wasn't until
he called me from a jail cell that I learned what he had been
dealing with.

I remember a distinct change in how I felt about drug use
once I recognized that my brother had been living this whole
time dealing with something I just didn't even know about.
And how hard it was. It's the point Bryan Stevenson[1] always
makes about being proximate. It just opened my eyes. Because
usually, as the prosecutor, you argue that a positive drug test
is evidence that someone charged with a crime can't abide by
the court's orders if they're on release pending trial. And I just
completely saw it differently.

The other life experience that also influenced me happened
when I was in high school. My father was a victim of a violent
robbery that left him with a severe closed-head injury. It
changed everything—his life, all of our lives. We had to
watch and assist as he had to learn how to walk and talk and
everything again. There were huge ramifications for all of us
emotionally, economically, and in other ways. My father still
lives with some of the effects from that injury today.

It was a huge harm, but the system wasn't the solution. There
wasn't anything the system could offer that was going to
address this new reality for us. That was always in the back
of my mind when so much of what we did as prosecutors was
done in the name of "justice," as in—*This is how we get justice for*

1   Founder of the Equal Justice Initiative

victims. But I was well aware of what it feels like to be on the other end and see the ramifications of violent crime that leads to serious harm.

I knew from my own practice that what you're told to do is get a conviction. Which means that survivor, that victim, is, unfortunately, a piece of evidence that you need to prove your case. As a prosecutor, you're *not* focused on real repair—what victims' needs are and how you get safety for them. You're just trying to make sure they show up for the grand jury and for trial, sometimes against their will. So I saw how the system, in many ways, can cause victims to be manipulated and actually further traumatized and further harmed.

This isn't something I've talked a lot about publicly, but my own father was a victim of another robbery in later years. I had been a prosecutor for a while—and he was getting these calls from the police department to come in, and they wanted him to testify. I said, "Daddy, they can't keep you safe. I don't think that's a good idea. You shouldn't go in." I felt like him showing up at some proceeding could potentially further endanger him. So, here I am, a prosecutor, telling my own father: Don't show up. Don't participate. The irony and the hypocrisy in that is real.

I wrestled with it, for sure, because I recognize I'm literally telling my father the opposite of what I do in my own cases. But I also knew I was in a federal system, even though I was prosecuting local cases, where we have more resources. We *could* do more for people who need services or who truly want to testify and take steps for their protection. I still had my own cases where there were people who did not feel safe and who would just rather not participate. And wherever I

could, I advocated for that. But I *was* in a jurisdiction where we regularly sought material witness warrants, which are warrants for arrest when a witness fails to appear for court or grand jury. You know, there are many bad things in the way the system operates. For me, that's probably one of the worst.

I thought that the ways we were trying to get justice were basically the right ways—just applied disproportionately and unfairly. I thought, especially early on: *I can come with a different set of experiences and be one of the power holders to at least try to use that power more fairly. To get justice for victims by getting that conviction and that sentence.* I also believed it was important that some of those decisions be made by someone who saw the people on the other side of those decisions as people. Because, in DC, certainly at the time I was there, it was primarily Black men that came through the system. And it was clear to me, even from the language used in the hallways, that the dehumanization was real. That they were not just "defendants." They were referred to as all kind of other things less than defendants. But I knew that any of those men could be *my* cousin, *my* uncle, *my* brother.

I remember a particular case I had probably in my second year, where I was told to charge a young man who was probably 19 with misdemeanor sexual abuse. That charge is kind of a catch-all that's often used when you can't prove a felony case or any kind of inappropriate touching. But it carried as part of its penalty that you have to register as a sex offender.

This was a case where he and the girl he was messing around with were caught. Her mother found the pictures in the girl's phone. She was 15. She was there with two other girls who were 16—16 being the age of consent. He was still in high

school even though he was 19. The fact that we were trying to charge him and would also require him to be registered as a sex offender was unconscionable to me.

I can remember being ready to quit. If I couldn't find a way to prevent this young man's life from being devastated, I wasn't going to be part of it. It was the first time I had ever really thought about quitting a job. But I went to some senior prosecutors and got their take on it—Black prosecutors, by the way. Because this was a young Black man. It was a young white girl.

Then I took my decision not to pursue this harsh punishment to my supervisor, who was a white woman. She wasn't happy about it, but she let me offer a plea to simple assault, which made him eligible for diversion so that ultimately, he would not have a record.

That was one that definitely stood out to me. I knew: *This is not fair.* We would have ruined his life just by him being a kid with other kids. All because the mom found her daughter's pictures in her phone and marched her down to the police station determined to file charges.

As you get a little older, you get a little more sure of who you are and what you believe. By the time I was more senior in the office, people knew who I was. My supervisors kind of expected that here I come again with a case I'm going to fight about and push hard against. But I definitely don't want to make it seem as if, *Oh, I was basically a public defender in the prosecutor's office.* I wasn't. I was prosecuting cases. There are still people in prison today because I helped put them there. That is something I reckon with and deal with.

I think about how they're going to be there for a long time. What that means for their family members. Is there something that could have been done differently?

There are lots of examples, unfortunately, like that, where I know I did what was my job at the time. And, at the time, felt like I was on the right side. I knew victims who had been pretty traumatized from having guns pointed at them and even worse for those who had been shot or stabbed. And this was, quote, unquote, our way of getting justice for them.

I did Title 16[2] cases where young people are charged as adults for violent crimes. When someone's been harmed you make all of those usual justifications. But, at the end of the day, they were kids. I certainly have a very different view now, especially with what we now know about brain science. Essentially, we should be thinking very differently about how we approach youth and young adults in response to harm they've caused. But, yes, I had those cases. I charged them and prosecuted them. But in hindsight, I now know better and just think all of those policies should be revisited and drastically changed.

But when you know better, you try to do better. So how do I now use the experience, the opportunities, the exposure to rectify harm? I contributed to this. I was a part of the system for a long time. So what can I do to help make it better and to make sure that we're doing things differently? That certainly motivates me in doing the work that I do now to take those learnings back into the environments where prosecutors are operating today. Building something for prosecutors to do the job differently. To recognize and attack all the things that I

2   Title 16 refers to the DC code that states that juveniles can be charged as adults.

struggled with in my time doing this job. Not just case-by-case, but to now help change systems.

Certainly, my deepest learning came after I stepped *away* from the office and came to the Vera Institute of Justice and really immersed myself in learning the history of the system and things that were just not taught in school. I came to truly understand the direct connection between our legacy of slavery and what we see in our system. For me, once I really learned that historical context, then it all made sense. The system isn't broken. Actually, it's functioning just as it was intended. That requires something so different from us. When you understand that this is a deeply rooted, intentional way of operating that has existed *since* the 13th Amendment, that requires us to truly think about dismantling. And how do we rebuild something in its place that's not rooted in the control and oppression and killing of Black people? Because that's what the system is rooted in.

My hope is that we're moving away from some of that. Even the hardest core prosecutor will admit that they know in their violent crime cases the person who's done this harm has usually been harmed from trauma that started from a very early age. It's not just that people wake up one day and decide, *I'm just going to go do something awful and cause a lot of harm to someone.*

There's a lot of harm *done* to people before they get to that point. So I do hope, at least, that there's some softening around how do we really get justice, and how do we define it differently, and how do we truly center the needs of survivors and victims in ways the traditional system hasn't? So that we can meet this moment where, as a country, we're reckoning with issues of race in ways that we haven't before. You know, usually, prosecutors

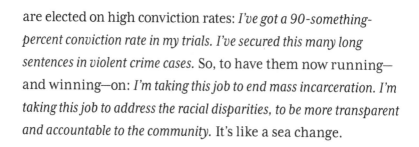

are elected on high conviction rates: *I've got a 90-something-percent conviction rate in my trials. I've secured this many long sentences in violent crime cases.* So, to have them now running—and winning—on: *I'm taking this job to end mass incarceration. I'm taking this job to address the racial disparities, to be more transparent and accountable to the community.* It's like a sea change.

It's exciting to be part of making that vision real. When you have a robust declination policy where prosecutors are saying, *I'm not charging cases that are clearly because someone has a mental health issue, or is struggling with substance abuse, or is poverty-related*—that's a significant impact on someone's life. When they say, *I'm not going to ask for cash bail because I recognize money has nothing to do with dangerousness or the ability to return to court. If you need to be detained, then we need to have a hearing and a judge needs to make a finding.*

We are overcoming a long history of dehumanization of Black people that we've never reckoned with since the very foundation of our country. That's not an easy challenge. We're trying to push a boulder up a hill, you know? We can lean in at this moment while people are reading books and having conversations and trying to learn more. We can decide, as a country, who we want to be. Are we going to let the boulder roll back down the hill? Like we did after Reconstruction? After the civil rights movement? Or are we going to actually try to push the boulder over and have a new vision of what justice can be and who we are as a country? That's my hope in this moment.

This conversation piece has been edited since its original October 2021 publication.

A Reverse Sting

by Brandon H.

From across the seas we came
Enslaved on ships in chains
From slave plantation workers
Whipped, lynched and shamed
From across the seas we emerged
To entrepreneurs and fame
Teachers, Olympians and world leaders
A conquering flame
On Plymouth rock we stand
From across the seas we came
Work still to be done
Look how life has changed
From across the seas we emerged
Still we remain
A forever burning flame
From across the seas we came

Drumming Pains

by Tony

Listen to the pains of the beating drum
Mental Anguish
Ba.dum.ba.dum.dum
The sounds of a mind taking a beating
Sent to the ghettos, stripped from their kingdom
Bum.Dum.Ba-dum.bum
It's hide screams at every beat that comes
Ba.Dum.Ba.Dum.Dum
Rhythm & Blues; Pain never sounded so good
Embracing our culture, if they only understood
Ba.dum.Ba-dum.bum
Heavy bass on the beat soothes my mind on these streets
Nighttime, my baby went to sleep on my heartbeat
BA.BUM.BA.BUM.BA.BUM
Voluptuous hips rock to the heavy beat of the soul
Synchronized to the sound of its own
Whum-bum.Whum.bum.bum
A powerful nation, the beat of its throne
An unstoppable machine feared cuz they know
Ba.dum.Ba.dum.Bum
That soulful beat passed down for centuries
Voices are heard from lungs never empty – full of life
These drumming pains have history
Ba.dum.Ba-dum.Bum
So next time you hear heavy bass or that bellowing drum
Listen to its spirit; that beat where I come from
Ba.dum.Ba.dum.Bum

Black, Gifted & Proud

by Davon B.

Since I'm Black and considered 1/3 of a man
They feel I can only relate to crime
My physical imprisonment is a tactic
To conceal thoughts produced by my creative
Innovative strength of mind
I'm united as one man
& hope my Brothers and Sisters will unite as one Klan
Stripped of our nationality and culture
Only to become ancestors to no land
My pigmentation is a pig temptation
To annihilate our race and uplift America
To a white man nation
The truth is basic
Only seek by those willing to see
If you choose to face it you'll learn
What seems to still be confusing to me
One nation under God
Was facilitated by a façade
To weaken our defenses from simply
Oppressing the odds
Now who's in charge
The last decision
Is OURS
As a whole we must proclaim
We're Black, Gifted and Proud.

Haiku
by John

Brown enough to hate
Love me, I am a person
I will love you back

The Labels of My Life

by Quenten

Precious

Precocious

Mischievous

Rambunctious

Spoiled

Rebellious

Hard Headed

Procrastinator

Daydreamer

Outspoken

Charismatic

Manipulative

Intelligent

Friend

Comrade

Sweetheart

Colored

Negro

Black

Afro American

African American

N*gger

Graduate

Airman

Civilian

Muslim

Christian

Five Percenter

Son

Brother

Uncle

Nephew

Grandson

Teammate

Leader

Follower

Suspect

Perpetrator

Criminal

Inmate

Convict

Felon

Mentor

Inspiration

Achiever

Overcomer

Some labels are permanent and others come and go. But what is most important is what you choose to lay claim to and the ones you don't. And even more important than them all is how you will define your life by the character of your heart, what you call yourself will determine what you think, feel, say and do.

Halim
(conversation)

When I was little, my parents were married and I had a good, wholesome household. But my childhood is kind of like BC and AC—Before Crack, and After Crack. I was six years old when I became aware that my father was smoking crack. So many parents in the community had the sickness. When I saw my father's life crumble under the weight of his addiction, and the gun violence that came with it, it just really robbed me. It took my innocence.

My life became very violent. I got lost in the streets. Back then, we didn't have Jay-Z and Diddy, you know, Barack Obama. People that looked like me that were successful. Even the mayor was allegedly smoking crack. We all wanted to get out of the murder capital of the country. The only way we saw to be successful was to sell crack. At first, you don't see the life sentences, the deaths from gun violence. You're just drawn in. It pulls you in and swallows you slowly. I became cold. I was addicted to marijuana, I drank alcohol. I didn't care about school. All I wanted to do was sell drugs all day and engage in robberies. I thought I was fearless. Young kid, thought I was a man. But really, I was *fearful* because I was living my life to impress other people.

When I was 16, I was charged as an adult as an accomplice to felony murder. All of my friends had been through DC jail. It was like a rite of passage, unfortunately. It was expected. The main thing I remember thinking in the courtroom was, *Man, let's just get it over with!* That's how immature I was. I was sentenced to 40 years to life. It didn't faze me at all. They sent

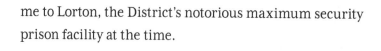
me to Lorton, the District's notorious maximum security prison facility at the time.

This older guy at Lorton used to hear me rapping, and one day when I was 17, he asked if I'd ever heard of George Jackson. I said, "Nah, but I heard of *Michael* Jackson. I heard of *Tito* Jackson." He just said, "Here, read this book." He gave me *Soledad Brother: The Prison Letters of George Jackson*. I will never forget reading that book for the first time. Jackson was just a teenager like me when he came to prison. He had a life sentence but he was able to write a book that people all over the world read. Through that book, I seen the power of the pen. You can literally reach outside your confines and create a movement. I decided, this is my path. This is how I'm going to get out.

My life began to change. I educated myself. I read everything I could get my hands on. I read about world history, philosophy, political science, and I read about every world religion. I started reaching out to people on the outside. I wrote to everybody: presidents, CEOs, kings, deans of universities. I told my story and let them know I was committed to my own personal redemption and helping others. I would ask them to mentor me. And a lot of them wrote back. Professors—people like Henry Louis Gates, Jr.—started sending me books and magazines. And I wrote. I went from writing rap to writing poetry. I published my first book of poems in 2005. I've published a total of 11 books.

The more I read and the more I wrote, the more I realized how externally driven I had been in society. I had forsaken my education to be a street gangster because I was seeking praise from my community. I made a commitment that I would no longer measure my life by other people. Reading and writing helped me to validate and love myself.

I learned how to find joy in the now—even when the "now" was in prison. I regained an appreciation for human life. Not just remorse for my crime, but remorse for all of the bad decisions I've ever made—selling drugs to people, profiting off of peoples' addictions, even littering. I developed my faith in Islam, but it was more than just a religious turning point. It was the understanding that all life is sacred because it is all interconnected. It's a process that is still evolving in me. It's a complete appreciation for life. I just don't know if a 16-year-old can understand that. I know I haven't met any that truly can, have you?

I don't believe my sentence was unfair. What was unfair was not having a process to have a review at some point to see, have I changed? You know, have I developed remorse and contrition, and am I suitable to try again as an adult citizen? I was a child. I stood 5'1" and weighed 110 lbs. My body swam in a prison jumpsuit. It just wasn't right to do a child like that. You got to give a child another look.

When I heard about the Incarceration Reduction Amendment Act, I felt it was vindication for what I had been telling people for years. This legislation would allow people who committed serious crimes before their 18th birthday to petition the court for resentencing after they served at least 15 years. People thought I was crazy, but I wrote to every single member of the DC Council. And when the opportunity came, I wrote testimony. I fought for it. I willed it. I just knew they would give us a chance to have our sentences reviewed. And in 2016, I saw my way out. The bill passed.

In March 2019, Halim was resentenced under DC's Incarceration
Reduction Amendment Act. He was released after serving 22 years in
adult prisons beginning at age 16. Halim has been awarded the Halcyon
Arts Lab and Echoing Green fellowship awards. He has written and
published 11 books of poetry and nonfiction, and is a professional artist.
Halim lives with his wife and their young daughter. His purpose is to
travel and share his message of love with the world through spoken word
and visual arts.

Writing My Way Out

by Makkah Ali

Peace and blessings, love and light, to overcome this plight is why I write

I am made free through my words without a doubt

Before I ever die inside, let me live forever through my work

They say life is priceless but do a price check

How much is an inmate worth?

Living within a system that profits from wrongdoings and mistakes

Writing my wrongs through poems is my one escape

Now literally I put my life on these lines

Because in this precious life

You never know when you'll run out of time

"Oh my," I ask, "Where has all the time went?"

It's now being spent writing my way out of confinement

These nights are young while these days are old

Writing my way out is the one way my story is being told...

At the moment

Writing my way out

Speak, Child, Speak

by Malcolm

To my daughter, Imani

Speak, child, speak
hold not your tongue because the question that you ask
the answer that it brings may be the solution that saves us all

Speak, child, speak
because ignorance is not bliss
it is apathy to the mind
it is the residue of stagnant thoughts that destroy itself fully
with the passions of time
& stagnation is death to young & old minds

Speak, child, speak
your voice may be the one that touches the world & shapes reality
into a paradise that women, men, & children may grow & peacefully live in

Speak, child, speak
because my voice is old & un-remembered
it is the weeping in the bowels of coffin ships & it is the creak of rope & wind
& silent kingdoms swaying in a sultry southern breeze
it is the shackles of falsehoods binding me to inferior thoughts of mental
    slavery
it is the sound of a fast life lived & lost in courtrooms
silently weeping in cells trying to escape my self-created hell

Speak, child, speak
because you are the Grace of God & the Dreams of a Nation

SPEAK, CHILD, SPEAK

Acknowledgments

This book would not exist without the incredible work and dedication of all of our members and staff, who contributed in immeasurable ways. Our members not only wrote the majority of this book, but they also shaped the vision for this book and weighed in on countless decisions throughout this process. This book belongs to the entire Free Minds community.

Special thanks to photographer and author KK Ottesen for donating her time and immense talent to this project. We also thank Ricardo Levins Morales, a profound social justice artist, for bringing the Free Minds members' vision of *When You Hear Me (You Hear Us)* to life via his cover art.

We are grateful for the generous financial support from both individuals and institutions that make our work possible. Free Minds receives and has received funding from the following:

Arabella Advisors
Clark-Winchcole Foundation
Clausen Family Foundation
Crowell & Moring Foundation
DC Commission on the Arts and Humanities
DC Office of Victim Services and Justice Grants
Elkes Foundation
Georgetown Presbyterian Church
Global Fund for Children
Greater Washington Community Foundation
Harman Family Foundation
The Herb Block Foundation
The Humanities Council of Washington, DC
The International Monetary Fund

John Edward Fowler Memorial Foundation

Lainoff Family Foundation

Mid-Atlantic Arts Foundation

Miller & Chevalier Charitable Foundation

Miller-Wehrle Family Foundation

Morris & Gwendolyn Cafritz Foundation

The PECO Foundation

Philip L. Graham Fund

Public Welfare Foundation

Rossetter Foundation

Rotary Foundation of Washington, DC

Share Fund

The SuPau Trust Private Foundation

Takoma Foundation

Wapakoneta Area Community Foundation

This book is made possible in part by a grant from HumanitiesDC, a partner of the DC Commission on the Arts and Humanities. The views presented in this book do not necessarily represent the views of HumanitiesDC.

Free Minds thanks the DC Department of Corrections and Department of Youth Rehabilitation Services who have continued to support our work.

About Free Minds Book Club & Writing Workshop

Free Minds Book Club & Writing Workshop uses the transformative power of reading and creative writing to amplify the voices of individuals directly impacted by mass incarceration. Free Minds provides peer mentoring and supportive programming to members throughout and after their incarceration, connecting them with resources to create personal and societal change. Through the literary arts, workforce development, trauma healing, leadership training and advocacy, Free Minds members become social justice leaders working to end mass incarceration. Since its founding in 2002, Free Minds has worked with over 1,500 incarcerated and formerly incarcerated individuals with its services.

Free Minds engages members through four phases:

- Jail Book Club: Book clubs and writing workshops at the DC Jail and juvenile detention center, providing therapeutic group sessions where members participate in guided meditation, community building activities, book discussions, and creative writing exercises. Free Minds provides tailored services to meet the unique and underserved needs of incarcerated Spanish-speakers with the Mentes Libres ("Free Minds" in Spanish) Book Club and incarcerated women with the Women's Book Club.

- Prison Book Club: Free Minds provides crucial support to members incarcerated in over 110 federal prisons across the country due to DC's non-state status. Free Minds maintains long-distance correspondence by sending books, letters, postcards, birthday cards, the Free Minds Connect magazine, and encouraging feedback on members' poetry from diverse volunteers across the country.

- Reentry Book Club: Free Minds provides holistic support to members returning home through a job readiness apprenticeship, jobs and educational placements, book discussions and writing workshops, a peer support training program, trauma-informed therapy, a Black History learning group, and a life stories project. Members lead an advocacy team and leadership development programming to create system change.

- On the Same Page: Free Minds members home from prison connect with diverse audiences from the community through our racial equity education and peacebuilding initiative. Free Minds members visit schools, universities, juvenile detention facilities, and community groups as Poet Ambassadors to share their life experiences and poetry. Participants share their perspective on the root causes of, and solutions to, youth incarceration—a dialogue that promotes healing and nonviolence. Free Minds also brings our members' poetry and personal stories to the community through Write Night events. Volunteers gather to read poetry, meet the Poet Ambassadors, and write feedback for the incarcerated poets.

Free Minds Book Club & Writing Workshop is a 501(c)(3) nonprofit organization. For more information or to make a tax-deductible donation, visit our website at freemindsbookclub.org.

Other Young Adult Titles from Shout Mouse Press

How to Grow Up Like Me, Ballou Story Project (2014)

Trinitoga: Stories of Life in a Roughed-Up, Tough-Love, No-Good Hood,
Beacon House (2014)

Our Lives Matter, Ballou Story Project (2015)

The Untold Story of the Real Me: Young Voices from Prison,
Free Minds Book Club & Writing Workshop (2016)

Humans of Ballou, Ballou Story Project (2016)

The Day Tajon Got Shot, Beacon House (2017)

Voces Sin Fronteras: Our Stories, Our Truths,
Latin American Youth Center (2018)

I Am the Night Sky: … & other reflections by Muslim American youth,
Next Wave Muslim Initiative (2019)

The Ballou We Know, Ballou Story Project (2019)

They Called Me 299-359, Free Minds Book Club & Writing Workshop (2020)

Shout Mouse Press is dedicated to centering and amplifying the voices of marginalized youth (ages 12+) via writing workshops, publication, and public speaking opportunities. Our work provides a platform for these young people to tell their own stories and, as published authors, to act as leaders and agents of change.

For the full catalog of Shout Mouse books, including illustrated children's books, visit shoutmousepress.org.

For bulk orders, educator inquiries, and nonprofit discounts, contact orders@shoutmousepress.org.

Books are also available through Amazon.com, select bookstores, and select distributors, including Ingram and Follett.